For my mother and father.

And with love and gratitude to Nigel,
who is my most supportive fan.

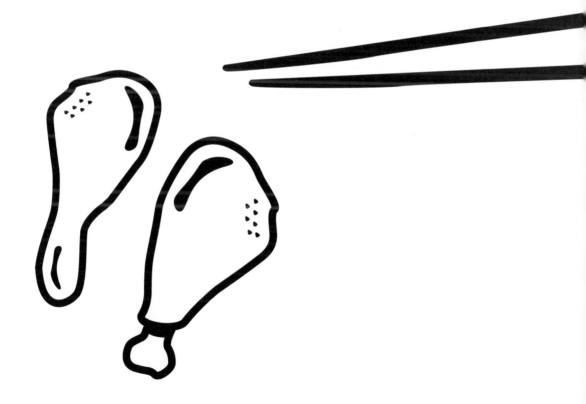

KUNG PAO &

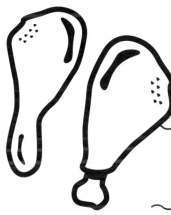

FRIED CHICKEN RECIPES FROM
EAST AND SOUTHEAST ASIA

BEYOND

SUSAN JUNG

Hardie Grant

QUADRILLE

PHOTOGRAPHY BY YUKI SUGIURA

Managing Director Sarah Lavelle
Commissioning Editor Stacey Cleworth
Designer Katy Everett
Photographer Yuki Sugiura
Photography Assistant Alexis Ko
Food Stylist Sam Dixon
Food Stylist Assistants Connie Simons and Kristine Jakobsson
Prop Stylist Max Robinson
Head of Production Stephen Lang
Senior Production Controller Martina Georgieva

Published in 2023 by Quadrille
an imprint of Hardie Grant Publishing

Quadrille
52–54 Southwark Street
London SE1 1UN
quadrille.com

Cataloguing in Publication Data: a catalogue record for this book is
available from the British Library.

Text © Susan Jung 2023
Photography © Yuki Sugiura 2023
Design © Quadrille 2023

ISBN 9781787139336

Printed in China

CONTENTS

INTRODUCTION

Is there any omnivore out there who doesn't like fried chicken?

When I was the food and wine editor for the *South China Morning Post* in Hong Kong, a position I held for close to 25 years, I wrote about a wide variety of dishes for my weekly recipe column. Invariably, the recipes that received the most online clicks and feedback from the readers were the ones for fried chicken. My editors sent requests: 'More fried chicken recipes, please', but how many could I publish each month without being repetitive? However, as I talked to friends living in East and Southeast Asia and they reminisced about the fried chicken dishes they knew and loved, I began to realize that there are a vast number of dishes I could write about.

In this part of the world, fried chicken goes far beyond the '11 herbs and spices' of the famous American fast food chain. Here, fried chicken can be flavoured with soy sauce, fish sauce, five-spice or Sichuan peppercorns – seasonings that are now familiar to much of the world. But they can also use lesser known ingredients such as fermented shrimp paste, curry leaf, salted egg yolks, or myriad types of chilli pastes. I originally wanted this book to be representative of all of Asia, but due to the sheer volume of dishes, my culinary borders had to stop somewhere. I realized I couldn't include the fried chicken of Central, South, North and West Asia, or the book would have been twice as long. I also didn't include fried chicken recipes from East and Southeast Asian countries I haven't visited, such as Myanmar, Mongolia and Cambodia.

My love for fried chicken started when I was young, when I was growing up in my parents' home in Monterey Park, California. My mother made fried chicken wings that my brothers and I loved so much we would ask for them on our birthdays, or on the rare occasions she asked us what we wanted for dinner. My Ah Ma and Ah Yeh – paternal grandmother and grandfather – immigrated to the United States from the village of Kow Kong, in southern China. For all the big Chinese holidays, we, and other Los Angeles-based families who hailed from the same village, would gather for a celebration lunch at the Kow Kong Benevolent Association building in downtown LA's Chinatown. The menu never changed: chow mein, fried chicken and this bright pink artificial-tasting punch fancied-up with a block of raspberry sherbet that melted slowly in the warm liquid (even as a child I thought the concoction was disgusting). My father was in charge of the chow mein, while one 'uncle' (the term we children used for all the older men, even if we were unrelated) made the fried chicken. He used only the drumsticks and thighs – which all of us preferred over the chicken breast – and the dish was similar to the Chinese–American fried chicken sold at the 'Chinese delis' (cooked food shops) in Chinatown and other areas of California with large Chinese populations. Unfortunately for everyone, this uncle was secretive – he kicked everyone (including my father) – out of the kitchen when he was cooking, so nobody knew why his chicken – deeply flavoured, and with a fantastically crunchy crust – was so much better than all other versions.

My love for fried chicken never ceased. When at university, I often took a break from studying by cooking for friends, and they loved it when fried chicken was on the menu. I always made too much – enough for plenty of leftovers – because eating a midnight snack of cold fried chicken while studying for exams is one of life's great joys. In Hong Kong, while living in a small flat with a kitchen so tiny there was no space for an oven (and even the fridge was in the living room), I served huge platters of fried chicken for Christmas, instead of the usual roast turkey. In my travels around East and Southeast Asia, I searched for new-to-me fried chicken dishes at hawker centres and food markets. I even love fast food fried chicken. My favourite is Jollibee – a chain from the Philippines, but I am happy to eat McDonald's wings, or Popeye's spicy version.

I hope you love fried chicken as much as I do, and that in this book, you can find recipes that will satisfy your cravings.

THE EAST & SOUTHEAST ASIAN PANTRY

The East and Southeast Asian section of a supermarket is no longer considered an 'exotic' aisle filled with 'mysterious' bottles and packages to examine and wonder about. Thanks to chefs who refuse to tone down their dishes in order to cater to palates unfamiliar with their cuisine, excellent cookbooks that focus not on entire countries but on specific regions of a country, and the public's willingness to taste new foods (new to them, anyway) and then attempt to make them in their own kitchens, open-minded cooks are seeking out ingredients from all over the world. Cooks don't have to settle for canned water chestnuts or canned bamboo shoots – if the fresh vegetables aren't sold in the supermarket, some intrepid farmer is growing them for the local farmers' market. And what you can't find locally is often available online.

But even when ingredients overlap in cuisines, they are not necessarily the same. Fresh local chickens – considered a special treat due to their price in other parts of the world – are sold at wet markets and supermarkets in Hong Kong, and the price is fair – about HK$70 for a bird (although certain breeds beloved by chefs can sell for more than four times that much). Those who are familiar only with the enormous chickens with oversized breasts that are mass produced by multinational corporations might think that Hong Kong chickens are scrawny. It's true that they are only about 1.2kg (2lb 9oz) each, but the meat is firmer and far more delicious than an oversized bird. Soy sauce and fish sauce are being used outside East and Southeast Asian kitchens as chefs realize that these ingredients can add a good dose of umami to even non-Asian dishes, but what is available to them in their parts of the world is nowhere near as varied as what we can buy in just about any local supermarket.

In this chapter, I've written about ingredients used in at least two of the recipes. Information about the more unusual ingredients, such as salted eggs and preserved beancurd (see pages 50 and 86), is covered in the recipes that use them.

CHICKEN

You can't have a fried chicken cookbook without writing about the chicken, and here's where I am supposed to tell you that you should use only free-range, locally raised (from wherever you happen to be living), fresh birds. In an ideal world, where everyone is making enough money and can therefore afford the higher cost of this kind of product (and I'm not complaining about the price, because chicken farmers deserve to make a decent living, too), that's what we would be using.

But it's not an ideal world, and the reality is that frozen chicken is usually more affordable – and it's what I used for most of these recipes. I do seek out producers that raise their chickens without antibiotics or added hormones. And I avoid the big-name American brands for both chilled and frozen birds, because commercially reared USA chickens are bred not for their taste and texture, but to be large and fast growing, and to have very disproportionately sized breasts.

Try frozen chicken parts from different brands to see which ones offer the best quality in your price range. Depending on the producer, a 1kg (2lb 4oz) bag of mid-joint chicken wings can have 16–24 pieces. A boneless thigh can weigh from about 85–135g (3–4¾oz), while breasts can weigh from about 150g (5½oz) to a whopping 350g (12oz). For my recipes, it's better to use chickens – or chicken parts – that are of reasonable size.

THE BASICS

Salt

This is the most important seasoning in all cooking, not just for fried chicken. Most of these recipes – and all of the chicken breast ones – call for pre-salting the chicken, usually before adding the marinade. I do this so the salt can penetrate into the meat, and, if left long enough, it also slightly firms up the texture. For boneless pieces of dark meat (drumstick or thigh), I usually pre-salt for at least 15 minutes, but for breasts and larger pieces of bone-in chicken, I like to salt for a minimum of 30 minutes.

It's also important to use the correct amount of salt, so the dish doesn't end up over- or under-seasoned. I weigh the meat, then add salt in a certain percentage: usually 1%, but it can be 0.5% (if the marinade has a lot of sodium) or up to 1.5% (if the recipe doesn't have much other seasoning).

Volume measurements of salt vary greatly in weight, depending on whether you're using salt flakes or grains; grains are dense and therefore heavier. But the weight also depends on the size of the flakes or grains. A level teaspoon of what is commonly used as table salt (very small grains) weighs about 5.7g, while the same volume measurement of large-flaked sea salt (such as Maldon) can weigh about 3.4g.

The salt I use most is often labelled as coarse kosher salt, and the flakes are larger than table salt, but smaller than Maldon or Diamond Crystal (another popular brand of kosher salt). Morton's might be the most famous brand (at least in the United States of America), but there are other, similar types. I like it because with my measuring spoons, the salt pretty consistently measures out to 5g per teaspoon. If you're using a different type of salt and are reliant on teaspoons and tablespoons, you'll have to adapt the volume recipes on your own because 5g of your salt might not equal 1 teaspoon.

This is where I strongly recommend using a precision scale that can weigh as little as 1/100 of a gram (you should also have another scale that can weigh larger amounts). Most of these recipes call for 800g–1kg (1lb 12oz–2lb 4oz) of chicken, but I don't expect you to search the supermarket shelves or your bag of frozen chicken parts trying to find pieces that weigh exactly that amount. The recipe will still work if you use

827g (1lb 13oz) or 1.2kg (2lb 9oz), respectively, but you should use the correct amount of salt for that weight. Just use your calculator and multiply the amount of meat by 0.005, 0.01, or 0.015, depending on what the recipe calls for.

Whatever salt you use, please avoid the type with added iodine – it gives a metallic taste to foods.

Oil

The essential qualities to look for when choosing a frying oil are neutral flavour and a high smoke point – that's the temperature where the heated oil begins to emit a visible smoke. If you heat it too much beyond that point, the oil can catch fire. Choose an oil that has a smoke point of at least 200°C (400°F).

I tested all the recipes with corn oil because it's inexpensive and easily available. I also like peanut (groundnut) oil but avoid cooking with it in case any of my guests has a peanut allergy. Soybean oil, sunflower oil and rapeseed (canola) oil are fine, reasonably priced frying oils. I'd avoid using expensive oils that come only in small bottles – even if they can be used for frying, it doesn't mean you should.

Soy sauce

I am somewhat of a soy sauce obsessive, and on my shelves in Hong Kong are soy sauces from all over East and Southeast Asia. When I cook Chinese food, I reach for my favourite brands, Kowloon Soy or Yuan's, both of which are made in Hong Kong, but if I'm making Japanese, I might use white soy sauce (which is actually clear; it's good because it doesn't change the colour of food) or some other small-batch type that I bought on my travels. If I'm making a Korean meal, I use Korean soy sauce, when I make Filipino food, I use a Filipino brand. I also sometimes mix types of soy sauce, using different amounts of light soy sauce (so called because of the consistency and colour; it has nothing to do with calories or sodium content) with dark soy sauce (which is sweeter), depending on the final flavour I want.

But I don't expect you to be as obsessive as me, so I tested all of these recipes with the soy sauce that has penetrated the market almost everywhere: Kikkoman 'all-purpose seasoning'. It lacks the complexity of the more expensive types, and I encourage you to explore how much better some soy sauces can be. Kikkoman also makes higher quality soy sauces that you can buy in speciality shops. One big clue is the price – they are more expensive than the brand's all-purpose seasoning, and the writing on the label will (probably) be in Japanese only.

Rice wine

In all of these recipes, rice wine is used in small amounts and I doubt that anyone can taste the quality of what you use. Still, I use two types: sake (for Japanese dishes) and Shaoxing rice wine (for everything else). There's no need to use expensive junmai daiginjo sake, which has highly polished rice grains, because the subtleties would be lost in cooking. Just look for good-quality drinking sake without added alcohol.

For Chinese rice wine, avoid at all costs the 'cooking wines' that have salt added to them. Good-quality, reasonably priced Shaoxing rice wine is fairly easy to find in larger supermarkets and online. There's no need to use the aged stuff, which can be incredibly expensive.

Fish sauce

Not all fish sauces are created equal, and like soy sauce, the taste can vary from country to country, and from brand to brand. On my shelves, I have fish sauce from Thailand, Vietnam, South Korea, the Philippines and Italy. All are made using a similar technique: small, inexpensive fish (usually anchovies) are mixed with salt and left to ferment. The mixture is strained to extract the liquid, which is then aged before being bottled.

I use Thai or Vietnamese fish sauce in all of the recipes with the exception of the Filipino ones, where I used Filipino patis, which can be quite cloudy. Also, I use Korean anchovy sauce when I make Cucumber Kimchi (see page 168).

Vinegar

The vinegar section of my pantry shelves is second only to the soy sauces. I have at least 10 types: dark and light rice vinegar from Japan, Chinese brown, black, red and aged vinegar, and, from the Philippines, which produces some of the best, there's coconut,

palm, cane and a few others. If I had to choose just a few, I'd pick Japanese light rice vinegar, which doesn't discolour food the way dark vinegar can (and make sure it's real rice vinegar, and not rice-flavoured distilled vinegar), Chinese brown vinegar, and coconut vinegar.

Pepper

Many of these recipes call for finely ground white pepper, which has a hotter taste than black pepper. I buy this, rather than trying to make it myself. Commercially produced finely ground white pepper is completely pulverized, and I've never been able to achieve that with my pepper grinders or blenders. Buy it in small jars. Normally, with dried spices, I advise sniffing them to see if they are still potent, but this would be unwise with pepper.

For the recipes that call for medium-grind black and/or white pepper, freshly ground is more aromatic and flavourful than pre-ground.

Dried chillies and dried chilli flakes/powder

Most of my recipes that call for whole dried chillies are Chinese, so I choose an easily available Chinese variety: Tianjin (or Tien Tsin). This chilli – small, slender and glossy red – is quite hot. To use, rinse them briefly, then blot them dry. Tear the chillies in halves or thirds (depending on the size) and shake out and discard the seeds. When frying them, use a low–medium heat and watch them carefully: you want the colour to brighten, but don't want to scorch the chillies, which will give them an acrid taste.

For chilli flakes/powder, I have tried to keep it simple and limited myself to four: Japanese, Korean, Chinese and Thai.

Japanese shichimi togarashi isn't a pure chilli flake/powder; instead, it's a mix of seven ingredients (hence the 'shi' part in shichimi), only one of which is spicy. If you like chilli hotness, you might be disappointed with shichimi togarashi; instead, you should look for ichimi togarashi, which is made only of chillies.

Gochugaru – Korean chilli flakes – come in fine and coarse grind; buy the coarse variety, and look for a bright red colour. These chilli flakes are moderately spicy.

Tianjin chillies also come in fine and coarse grind, but for the recipes in this book, I use the fine powder. The powder absorbs humidity quite easily, so rather than decanting it into a jar, I keep it in the same airtight, sealable bag that it's sold in. Like the whole dried chillies, Tianjin chilli powder is quite spicy.

Thai chilli flakes are the coarsest of all – you can see the seeds and fibres. The colour is orange-red, and the flavour is very spicy. Because of the coarse texture, I use Thai flakes only when the grainy quality doesn't matter.

Gochujang

Korean fermented red chilli paste. Although its bright red colour might make you worry it's going to be incendiary, gochujang's spiciness is tempered by sweetness and a slight funkiness that comes from its fermentation process.

Doubanjiang

Sichuan fermented broad bean chilli paste. It's salty, spicy and umami.

Curry powder

These vary greatly in flavour, complexity and heat level. For all the recipes in this book, I used just one – Koon Yick Wah Kee, a made-in-Hong Kong brand, not because it is necessarily the best (although I like it), but for consistency. Choose a brand that you like.

Turmeric

This is the main flavouring and colouring in most curry powders. The bright orange rhizome is available fresh, dried and powdered. Most of these recipes use powdered turmeric, which is easier to find.

Turmeric is used as a natural dye, and it will stain work surfaces, cutting boards and your hands. I usually wear a disposable glove on my working hand when using a marinade that contains turmeric.

Sichuan peppercorns

Despite the name, Sichuan peppercorns (also called Sichuan pepper) are not related to the *Piper nigrum* plant that produces green, white and black peppercorns. Instead, it's a member of the citrus family. It has a strong, distinctive aroma, and a numbing, tingly effect on the tongue when you eat it. Only the husk part is used. Before using the peppercorns, put them on a white plate so you can examine them more easily, then pull out and discard the seeds (which are small and black), as well as any twigs. Look for a bright pink-red colour – if the peppercorns are dull and brown, they won't have much scent or flavour. They're usually heated before use – by toasting in a frying pan (skillet), or frying in oil, which brings out the aroma. Don't buy ground Sichuan pepper, because the flavour and aroma will fade quickly. Instead, toast the peppercorns and grind them just before using them. I like to use a suribachi (Japanese grinding bowl) to grind them.

Sesame seeds and sesame oil

Sesame seeds are sold white, tan or black, and raw or toasted. Because the fragrance of the toasted seeds dissipates quickly, it's best to toast them yourself, instead of buying the pre-toasted ones. The Japanese have special implements for toasting sesame seeds: either small, fine-mesh cages with a hinged lid, which you shake back and forth over an open flame (the lid prevents the seeds from popping out as they heat), or a round clay pot with an opening on top that you pour the sesame seeds into, and a hollow handle that you pour the seeds out of after toasting them. I take great pleasure in using my cage-type toaster – it's beautiful and well made, and I also use it when toasting Sichuan pepper, but in truth, it's not an essential piece of equipment. You can toast sesame seeds (and Sichuan peppercorns) in any frying pan: just pour the seeds into the unoiled pan and shake it back and forth over the heat. Watch them carefully because they can burn quickly.

The oil pressed from sesame seeds is very rarely used for frying (apart from some high-end tempura restaurants) because it's expensive and it has such a distinctive flavour. But it's one of the most fragrant, delicious oils to use in marinades and to finish dishes. I prefer the oil made from toasted seeds – it has a stronger flavour. Check the ingredients label to make sure that the oil contains only sesame seeds and hasn't been mixed with cheaper oils.

Chinese sausage

There are many varieties of dried sausages produced in China and Hong Kong. Lap cheong is the type that is most familiar to people in other parts of the world because the early Chinese diaspora was from southern China and they brought the production technique with them when they immigrated. Lap cheong are quite firm, and have a sweet, intense flavour. The ones I buy are around 60g (2oz) each, but they can vary in size, so I've given the amounts in weight, rather than the number of sausage links. They keep for several months in the freezer.

Fermented black beans

These small black beans pack a powerful umami punch when used in dishes. They are made by salting, fermenting and drying soybeans, which shrivels them and concentrates the flavour. They should be soaked in warm water for about 15 minutes before use.

Chinese mushrooms

China grows hundreds of varieties of edible mushrooms, including many that are associated with European cuisines, such as porcini, morels and chanterelles. When a recipe calls for Chinese mushrooms without specifying the type, it means dried shiitake mushrooms. They can vary greatly in price, depending on the quality. The best are evenly shaped, have thick caps, and have an attractive pale and dark flower pattern on the surface. Dried mushrooms should be soaked in cool water – not hot, which leeches out the flavour. They take several hours to fully hydrate – at least 3 hours, but often much longer. If I remember to plan in advance, I like to soak them overnight in the fridge. The water used to soak the mushrooms should be strained to remove any grit, then used in place of plain water in dishes.

Tamarind

There's no substitute for this tart, tangy fruit with a hint of sweetness. I buy jars of tamarind paste (which is more like a thick liquid, rather than a paste) because it's easy to use, but you can make your own with tamarind pulp, which is sold in small, heavy packets. To make tamarind paste, take some of the pulp, add an equal weight of hot water, then let it soak until the water is cool. Pour it through a sieve placed over a bowl and press on the pulp with the back of a spoon, to force the soft pulp into the liquid. Discard the fibres and seeds left in the sieve. Make more than you need for whatever recipe you use, because the leftover tamarind paste can be stored in the fridge for a couple of weeks.

Starches/coating mixes

In the West, the default flour is wheat flour whenever a recipe doesn't specify a type, but in East and Southeast Asia, the flour can be made of a variety of grains and ingredients, including rice, glutinous rice, corn, potato, sweet potato, tapioca, mung bean and water chestnut. I tested all of them for these recipes and selected just a few.

My favourite flours for both batters and for dredging are made from potato, sweet potato and tapioca. Water chestnut flour is excellent, too, giving a firm crunch, but it can be difficult to find and is expensive. I don't use this for batters, just for dredging. Depending on the brand (some of which call their products 'starch' instead of flour) and the ingredient it's made from, some of these flours are coarse, not powdery, and need to be processed further to make them more like a typical flour. It's easy to do – just empty a bag of flour (about 250g/9oz) into a food processor, cover it with a lightly dampened dish towel (to contain the fine powder) and turn on the motor. Process the flour until it's smooth and powder-like. I find I always have to do this with water chestnut flour, and sometimes with tapioca or sweet potato flours.

Panko isn't a flour, but it's listed here because it's another good coating for fried chicken. These light, flaky, dried breadcrumbs give a delicate crunch to fried dishes.

One of my favourite commercial coating mixes is Thai tempura flour, made by a company called Gogi. It fries up light and crisp and doesn't get soggy immediately. You can order it online, but I've given a recipe for a homemade coating mix (see page 162) that is just as good. And yes, it can be made gluten-free.

The basic ingredients in a coating mix – whether Gogi or homemade – are flours (two types), baking powder and salt. The coating mix is combined with an equal weight of liquid to create a batter – the amount of liquid can be adjusted depending on whether you want a thick batter or a thin one. But you mustn't forget to take into consideration the liquid in the marinade for the chicken. If it's a wet marinade, you might not add any water at all. Even when the chicken is seasoned with just salt, there will still be some liquid in the bowl. If you were to add a batter made from equal weights of coating mix and iced water, the liquid from the marinade would dilute the batter, making it too wet. I usually add just the minimal amount of iced water to the coating mix, add this to the chicken, then adjust, if necessary, by adding more water. If the batter is too thin, just mix in more coating mix.

FRESH INGREDIENTS

Garlic

Garlic cloves vary in size, which is why I often give a weight measurement instead of specifying a certain number of cloves. And when I do specify the number of cloves, I usually give a range, say 3–5. It depends on the size of the clove, and how much you like garlic. If you're a real garlic lover, you might be tempted to use a lot more than the recipe calls for, but don't use so much that all other flavours are obliterated.

Fresh coriander (cilantro)

People are familiar with fresh coriander leaves but might not be aware that the stems and roots are also edible and very intense in flavour. The roots – and about 2.5cm (1in) of the lower stems – are minced and/or pounded to use in curry pastes, marinades and seasoning blends. If the coriander you buy comes without the roots (which help the herb stay fresh for longer), use the coriander stems.

Spring onions (scallions)

Spring onions vary greatly in size and flavour. Some are sweet and mild, while others are very strong – chopping them can make your eyes water, in the same way that cutting an onion might. If the spring onions are very strong, soak them in iced water after slicing, shredding or mincing them, then drain them and pat them dry before use..

Chinese celery

Chinese celery looks like thin, elongated stalks of standard celery, but it's not as fibrous and the flavour is stronger. I usually pull off the leaves to use as a garnish (or mix into the dish at the last minute, so they wilt gently), and I tear the stalks into 5cm (2in) lengths, because tearing seems to make the vegetable more aromatic than when cut. When buying Chinese celery, look for firm, unshrivelled stalks with perky, unwilted leaves.

Ginger

Look for firm rhizomes that feel heavy for their size. Fresh ginger keeps for weeks at room temperature – it might shrivel a bit, but it's still fine to use – and you can also freeze it. For all these recipes, the ginger is peeled – use a small spoon to scrape off the papery skin.

Shallots

There are many types of shallots, just as there are many types of onions. For all the recipes in this book, buy the shallots with purple-ish skin sold in Asian supermarkets. After peeling shallots, rinse them briefly under cool water to rid them of any dirt or dust.

Fresh chillies

There are thousands of varieties of plants that belong to the capsicum family, which grow edible fruit ranging from the mild bell pepper to the super-hot types such as the Scotch bonnet, ghost pepper and Carolina reaper. I've limited myself to three types.

Bell peppers – I use only the red, orange or yellow ones. I dislike green bell peppers because they taste unripe – and that's because they are. Look for peppers with firm, unwrinkled, glossy skin.

Banana chillies – Named for their curved shape which makes them resemble (sort of) the fruit, these can range from mild to slightly hot. They're quite long – about 18cm (7in), but the width at the stem end can vary from about 1.25cm (½in) in diameter to about 8mm (⅜in). I prefer the slender ones because they look nicer when sliced, but the larger ones are fine, too. They're available in red or green.

Bird's-eye chillies – This photogenic chilli almost screams 'Thai cuisine' when you see it in the pages of cookbooks or food magazines. It's small, pretty, slender, glossy and very hot. Bird's-eye chillies are available red and green, but the recipes in this book use them at the red stage.

I remove the seeds from these chillies, but I'm not obsessive about taking out every last one. Instead of slicing them in half and scraping out the seeds, I 'seed as I go'. Start by slicing the chillies into thin rings, then when you get to about a third of the way up the chilli, squeeze the upper part and roll it back and forth between your thumb and forefinger – this loosens the seeds. Once you've sliced far up enough along the chilli, you can squeeze and shake out some of the seeds. Slice a bit more and squeeze and shake out more of the seeds, until you get to the stem end.

Galangal

Galangal is a rhizome that's used often in Southeast Asian cooking. It looks quite similar to ginger (and they're both in the same family) but the flavour is very different, and you shouldn't try to substitute one for the other. Unlike ginger, I don't peel it before using it. Galangal can be frozen.

Limes

Thai limes have a very different flavour from Persian limes, and they're what I used for all of these recipes. They're small, fragrant, and very juicy, as long as you cut them right – which most people don't. Instead of slicing into two halves or four wedges, the Thai lime should be cut into five pieces, which lets you extract the greatest amount of juice. Most of the seeds are concentrated at the centre of the fruit, so you want to cut around that. Make the first cut off-centre, so you have one, evenly shaped, circular piece. Then make three more cuts around the core, which, when you are finished with it, will be somewhat cuboid in shape.

Makrut lime leaves

Makrut lime leaves are incredibly fragrant and are the main part of the tree that's consumed – not the bumpy fruit. The leaves come in pairs and, when used in a marinade, need to be finely julienned, or else they're too tough to eat.

Lemongrass

Lemongrass is one of the most aromatic of seasonings. The long stalk is hard and fibrous, and for cooking, only about the lower 8cm (3¼in) can be used – and even then, it's very tough. Trim off and discard the hard part at the very base (where it was attached to the root) and pull off the dried-out outer layers. Use the flat side of a metal meat mallet to bash the length of the stalk, then cut it as thinly as possible. The top, inedible part of the stalk can be roughly chopped and used to make a lemongrass tisane (herbal tea).

SUPPLIERS

Nothing beats shopping in person, but for convenience – and for finding ingredients that may not be available at your local store – it's sometimes easier to let your fingers do the walking and let an online shop ship to you. If your pantry is bare of East and Southeast Asian ingredients, you may have to search on several online shops to get everything you need.

United Kingdom

souschef.co.uk

theasiancookshop.co.uk

waiyeehong.com

orientalmart.co.uk

thai-food-online.co.uk

United States

99ranch.com

hmart.com

justasianfood.com

chefshop.com

dainobunyc.com

EQUIPMENT

~~~~~~

None of these recipes require expensive equipment, nor anything that is very unusual. You don't need an electric deep-fat fryer, and nor would I use its opposite extreme, the air fryer (although I'm sure it's great for reheating many fried chicken dishes). If you have a fairly well-equipped kitchen, you probably have much of the equipment in this chapter.

Wok

This inexpensive pan is incredibly versatile and can be used for far more than just stir-fries and steaming. I love woks so much that I have four in different sizes, but the ones I use most are a large 35.5cm (14in) wok and a medium one that's about 25cm (10in). All of my woks are carbon steel, which I prefer over stainless steel or other metals because it's lightweight, distributes the heat evenly, and is quick to heat or cool down. If seasoned and cared for correctly, carbon steel also develops a non-stick patina. My woks have slightly flat bottoms, which makes them more stable when placed over burners.

When used for frying, the wok has important advantages over straight-sided pans. The sloped sides mean it's easier to see the food as it cooks; with straight-sided pans, you have to be standing right over them to see inside. The sloped sides also give a greater surface area for the oil. If you pour 600ml (generous 2½ cups) of cooking oil into a 20cm (8in) pan, the oil will be about 2.5cm (1in) deep. If the oil is poured into a 25cm (10in) wok, you have the same depth of oil at the deepest point, but the surface area is about 23cm (9in), which means you can fry a larger amount of food at one time. I use my medium wok for frying chicken, and the larger one for stir-frying, and I suggest you do the same.

To season a new wok, scrub it vigorously with hot, soapy water to remove the factory coating. Dry the wok over a medium–high heat, then, while it's still hot, rub cooking oil into the metal so it has a light but even film. Using the wok over and over again for deep-frying is the best way to build up the seasoning.

You can also use the wok as a makeshift steamer. Put a small round rack with low feet in the wok and place a dish of food on top. Pour some water into the base of the wok, bring to the boil, then put the cover on the wok and steam until the food is cooked.

Frying pan (skillet)

While I use a wok for about 90% of the fried chicken recipes, there are times when a frying pan (skillet) is better. I use it mostly for larger chicken pieces, such as bone-in drumsticks or thighs, or whole breasts or legs. I like a cast-iron skillet that's about 30cm (12in), but stainless steel is fine, too.

Straight-sided pot

I use a straight-sided pot for only one fried chicken dish: Nor Mai Gai (see page 139) – a tunnel-boned whole chicken. You need one that's about 24cm (9½in) wide and at least 15cm (6in) deep.

Infrared thermometer or oil/candy thermometer

I love my infrared thermometer and use it almost daily when I cook. You can buy one inexpensively at most well-equipped hardware stores, or more expensively at cookware stores. When it comes to deep-frying, the infrared thermometer is far safer to use than a probe-type thermometer, which leaves your hand very close to the bubbling hot oil. Candy/deep-fat thermometers – the type that you clip on to the sides of the pan – also work but are less convenient; they can get in the way, they take up space in the pan, you have to make sure the bottom of the probe is completely submerged in the oil, and, if it's made of glass, it can break.

Digital scales

I have two: one that uses increments of one gram, and can weigh up to 5kg (11lb), and a smaller, more precise scale that weighs as little as 1/100 of a gram. The latter is essential for measuring the correct amount of salt.

Timer

It's important to get the timing right when frying chicken. Believe me, I've tried counting using 'one one-thousand, two one-thousand', and it's nowhere near as accurate as using a timer or stopwatch.

Long chopsticks

If you're adept at using chopsticks, you'll find long cooking chopsticks (about 42cm/16½in in length) a lot more delicate and precise than kitchen tongs. I like two types: wooden chopsticks, and thin metal chopsticks with wooden handles.

Hand-held sieve (strainer)

I have several of these, with different-size mesh or holes. These make it easier to scoop small pieces of chicken out of the bubbling oil, instead of taking them out piece by piece. A sieve with a fine mesh can be used to strain oil. They should be shallow, rather than bowl-shaped.

Food processor/high-speed blender

I use the former for pulverizing certain types of starches: water chestnut flour and certain brands of sweet potato flour can be rough, rather than powdery. I use the high-speed blender for making spice pastes.

Pestle and mortar

For certain jobs, nothing can replace a pestle and mortar. While I use a blender, food processor or chopper for making sambals and chilli pastes, I use the pestle and mortar for small jobs, such as pounding garlic and coriander root to a paste before mixing the ingredients into a marinade.

I have two, but if I had to choose just one, it would be the heavy clay mortar purchased on a trip to Thailand. It's 16cm (6¼in) deep and weighs about 2.5kg (5lb 8oz), with a wooden pestle. I regret not buying an even larger one.

Suribachi and surikogi

The suribachi (grinding bowl) looks very much like a mortar, but the interior is ridged, rather than smooth. It's also used in a completely different way. In a mortar, ingredients are pounded in an up-and-down motion to crush them, but in a suribachi, the surikogi (pestle) is used in a circular motion to pulverize them against the ridges. I've heard people call the suribachi a 'sesame seed grinder' because often, that's what it is used for, but I also use it for crushing peppercorns, Sichuan pepper and other spices.

Ceramic oroshigane

The Japanese make different oroshigane (graters) for grating specific ingredients: there's a sharkskin one for wasabi, another type for daikon, and others for finely grating the aromatic zest of citrus. The one I use most often is a ceramic grater for grating ginger and garlic. It makes a smooth, fine, juicy paste that you can't get with a rasp-type grater.

Metal meat mallet (tenderizer)

I use the flat side of the mallet for bashing a stalk of lemongrass before slicing it, and for flattening chicken breasts, to even out the thickness.

Cooling racks

I very rarely use paper towels to soak up the oil of fried chicken, because it can make the coating soften or become soggy. Instead, I put the fried food on a cooling rack placed over a tray. I also use the same set-up for air-drying the coated, floured chicken before frying it, which helps to set the crust.

Spring onion (scallion) shredder

This is not essential, but you'll be thankful you have one when shredding a large quantity of spring onions. The 5–7 blades are very sharp and are drawn along the length of the spring onions to quickly shred them. Be sure to replace the guard (which comes with the implement) when not using the shredder.

Electric rice-cooker

You don't absolutely need a rice cooker but if you eat a lot of rice, you'll find it very useful. Of course, rice can be cooked in a pot on the stove top, or in a steamer, but an electric rice cooker is far easier. Even the most basic of rice cookers – the type with just one switch (on/off) – turn off by themselves when the rice is ready and will keep the rice warm. I call for a rice cooker in only one recipe – Nor Mai Gai (tunnel-boned chicken that's stuffed with glutinous rice, air-dried and fried, see page 139) but plain rice is a good, neutral accompaniment to many of these fried chicken dishes.

COOKING TECHNIQUES

The most important techniques to know about when making fried chicken are, of course, related to the frying. And before you ask, I didn't test any of the recipes in an air fryer. These recipes make a lot of fried chicken – most use 800g–1kg (1lb 12oz–2lb 4oz) of raw meat – and unless you have a commercial-sized air fryer, cooking in one would take too long. Besides, there are too many variables when using an air fryer.

Frying isn't nearly as scary or difficult as people think it is. Yes, you have to watch out for splatters, but that's true even if you are sautéing or stir-frying. Frying is an incredibly efficient way of cooking: the ingredient is surrounded by fat that's been heated to a temperature far above the boiling point, and the oil sets the crust so the flavours are locked in instead of leaching out, as they would be if you were cooking them in water. It's not as wasteful as you might think, because if you use the right pan (see the section on woks, page 16), you'll need only about 750ml (3¼ cups) of oil at a time. And the oil can be reused several times (again, more on that later).

There are many mistaken beliefs about frying. One is that foods absorb a lot of oil if fried at a temperature that's too low – many people think that it is anything below 160°C (320°F). I fried chicken at least once a day for several months, and often weighed the oil before and after frying. It's impossible to know exactly how much oil was lost to the inevitable splatters and how much of it was supposedly absorbed into the food, but there seemed to be no difference in before and after weights of the oil when I fried a batch of chicken between 140–150°C (284–300°F) and when I fried at 160°C (320°F) or higher. I know some chefs are experimenting with low-temperature frying – with oil heated to 120°C (250°F). That's not practical for home cooking, though.

Overheating the oil

Often, recipes instruct to heat the oil to a specific temperature and then fry at that temperature. But as soon as you add the ingredients, the oil temperature drops considerably – 20°C (68°F) or more. You need to heat the oil past the target frying temperature, so that after you've added the ingredient, the temperature drops to close to what you want it to be. For a target frying temperature of 160°C (320°F), heat the oil to 180°C (350°F) degrees; to fry at 170°C (340°F), heat it to 190°C (375°F). Be sure to adjust the heat as you're frying to maintain the correct cooking temperature.

The chicken should be at room temperature right before it's fried, to prevent the oil temperature from dropping even more.

Placing the food in the oil

Don't just drop the battered and/or starch-coated chicken into the hot oil – the oil will splash. Instead, place the chicken so part of it is just under the surface of the oil, then release it, so it slides into the oil, without splashing.

The amount of oil you have in your pan determines the amount of chicken you can fry at any one time. The chicken needs room to 'swim' in the oil: if you're frying too much at once, the pieces will crowd together, and won't get crisp.

When you first put the chicken in the hot oil, the pieces will drift together, and often, will stick to one another. Don't try to separate the pieces immediately because they will just drift together and stick again. Instead, wait for 30 seconds–1 minute for the crust to harden slightly, before using long chopsticks to gently tease apart the pieces. This doesn't work for oil-blanched dishes, or for chicken breasts, where the chicken is fried for as little as 30 seconds. For these recipes, put a smaller amount – about 150g (5½oz) or less – of the marinated chicken into the oil, then immediately use long chopsticks to separate the meat into individual pieces. Use a mesh or slotted ladle to scoop the pieces out of the oil, so they don't overcook.

Double-frying

Double-frying isn't a new technique, but it became better known with the increased popularity of Korean Fried Chicken (KFC) – it's what makes the chicken so crisp. Most of my recipes call for double-frying, with the exception being those that call for panko – the breadcrumb coating is sufficiently crisp after single-frying – and the ones where the chicken is oil-blanched, then stir-fried.

With double-frying, the first frying – at 150–160°C (300–320°F) – is to almost or fully-cook the chicken. The meat is rested briefly, before being re-fried at a slightly higher temperature (around 170–175°C/ 340–350°F), which crisps up the crust. During the second frying, you'll find that the chicken splatters more than with the initial frying, because there's more moisture on the surface.

Undercooking chicken breast

One of my goals in writing this book was to make chicken breast that is not dry, and I've succeeded. I achieve this by salting the breast and by slightly undercooking it. When the chicken is pulled out of the pan after the first frying, the exterior is about 160°C (320°F), or whatever the temperature of the oil was. With a brief resting time, the heat from the surface of the chicken has time to penetrate into the middle of the piece, taking it to a perfect doneness. For breasts, the second frying is very brief, so it doesn't cook much more – it's just long enough to re-crisp the crust.

BEFORE YOU FRY

Cutting the chicken into pieces

It's important to cut chicken into pieces that are as even as possible, so they cook in about the same time. Occasionally, I specify the size the pieces should be. There's no need to be obsessive about it and measure each piece with a ruler but try to get them as close as possible to the right size, or you might have to adjust the cooking times.

Butterflying chicken breasts

Chicken breasts are large and unevenly thick. To help the marinade flavour the chicken better, and to help the meat cook more evenly, I always butterfly the breasts, and also occasionally butterfly boneless thighs. Lay the breast on the cutting board. Use a very sharp chef's knife or cleaver to slice the breast at the thickest point, parallel to the cutting board. Cut almost through to the other side of the fillet, then open it like a butterfly. The breast can be cut into smaller pieces (for nuggets) or pounded lightly and used like cutlets.

Butterflying chicken thighs

To butterfly thighs, place the boneless thigh skin side-down on the cutting board. Working from the centre of the thigh, cut under the thickest parts of the meat, slicing at a slight angle towards the cutting board, and stopping before you reach the skin. You'll now have two flaps of meat attached close to the skin: open up the flaps and proceed with the recipe.

Salting the chicken

With many of my recipes – and always for the ones using chicken breast – I salt the meat before adding the other seasonings and/or marinade. I weigh the meat first, then add salt at the percentages of 0.005, 0.01 or 0.015, depending on how salty the marinade is. It doesn't need much time – for smaller pieces, just 15–30 minutes is usually sufficient for the salt to penetrate, and it also tenderizes the meat and makes it seem juicier when cooked – as long as you don't overcook it.

Marinating the chicken

Here's where the flavour comes in. Yes, you can have perfectly delicious chicken that's been seasoned only with salt and pepper, but with marinades, you can vary the flavour, making it spicy, sweet, tart, bitter, or any combination of these. To help the marinade get deep into the meat, I sometimes slash bone-in pieces, cutting down to the bone.

With most recipes, I give an indication of how long the meat should be marinated – from as little as 30 minutes and up to 24 hours. These are just guidelines – it's fine if you marinate for a shorter (although not less than 30 minutes) or longer time. If it works better for your schedule, the meat can be marinated in the fridge starting the night before or in the morning before work.

Unless you are living in an extremely hot climate, it's fine to marinate chicken at room temperature for up to about 3 hours (although use your judgement). For longer marination, put the chicken in the fridge. Be sure to let the chicken come to room temperature before cooking it.

Battering/coating the chicken

Frying chicken without some type of coating to protect it from direct contact with the hot oil results in meat that's tough and stringy. The exception is wings, which are fully encased in skin that serves as protection from the oil, but even with them, I almost always use a coating. At the very minimum, I dredge the marinated chicken in starch, preferring potato, sweet potato or tapioca flour over plain (all-purpose) wheat flour.

I've never understood why some recipes instruct you to throw away the marinade, then make a separate batter with starch and water. The marinade has a lot of flavour and using it as the liquid for the batter means the fried coating will be delicious.

If I want a thick, harder coating, I batter the chicken, then dredge it in starch. Occasionally – when I want to ensure the crunchiness will remain when the chicken is sauced – I batter it, dredge it in flour, let it rest so the coating sticks better, then dredge it again.

Air-drying

If you walk into a Chinese kitchen, especially one that serves Siu Mei (roasted meats), you'll often see chickens and other birds hanging over the stove top. These birds are being air-dried before they are cooked to order, because a drier surface crisps up better when fried or roasted.

I air-dry chicken before frying it. After dredging the chicken in flour, leave it for a few minutes on a cooling rack placed over a tray, to let the coating dry out slightly. You can tell when it's ready: the stark white coating will turn darker in spots.

Resting the meat

Chefs always talk about the importance of resting steaks or roasted meats, but the subject is never mentioned with fried chicken. The reason for resting larger cuts is to let the meat juices – which have been pulled to the surface while the meat is cooked – redistribute themselves deeper into the steak or roast meat, so they don't run out onto the cutting board when the meat is sliced or carved.

I let the meat rest between the first and second frying, because it allows the surface heat to permeate into the centre, giving it a more even doneness. How long you let the chicken rest depends on the size: for small pieces, just a few minutes is enough. Larger pieces need about 10 minutes. I also let the meat rest briefly just before serving it because when it's fresh out of the fryer, it's too hot to appreciate.

OTHER TECHNIQUES

Draining the chicken

Recipes often instruct you to drain the fried chicken on paper towels. I find this makes the bottom of the chicken soggy. Instead, I put the chicken on a cooling rack placed over a tray, so the air can circulate and the bottom of the chicken will be just as crisp as the top.

Oil-blanching

Oil-blanching is not a well-known technique, but it's common in the Chinese kitchen. Like blanching in water, the meat is dipped just briefly in hot oil, not to cook it, but to give it a smooth, velvety texture, giving rise to another term it's known as in English: velveting. The meat is then fully cooked later, often by stir-frying. Before being oil-blanched, the meat is mixed with a marinade that contains cornflour (cornstarch), or another starch, which helps to smooth the texture. (For more details, see page 145.)

Reusing the oil

Fresh oil that's straight out of the bottle is fluid, light and clear. Whatever you fry in the oil leaves behind some type of residue, which with repeated use, makes the oil break down – it becomes dark, thick and cloudy. If you use this old oil to fry, it makes food greasy and soggy, rather than light and crisp. You want to stop using the oil before it reaches this point.

Darkening alone isn't necessarily an indication that the oil is bad: it could be that you fried something that had a lot of spices in the marinade and the colour of them leached into the oil. The oil could still be usable, although I wouldn't reuse it to fry foods that have a more delicate taste.

You can extend the life of frying oil. While you're frying, if you see a lot of crumbs or residue at the bottom of the wok (or pan), use a hand-held fine-meshed sieve/strainer to scoop the residue out of the oil – do this each time you remove the fried chicken from the oil, before adding more. Then, keep a metal container, placed on a trivet or large cork coaster, next to the stove. Don't use a plastic container, which will melt, or anything that can break from the heat of the oil. After frying, use the mesh sieve/strainer to remove any larger bits of food floating in it. Strain relatively 'young' used oil (used once or twice) through the mesh sieve/strainer into the metal container – do this while the oil is still hot. Oil that's been used more than twice gets strained through the same sieve/strainer, but with the addition of a layer of paper towels to filter out the really fine particles. You have to use your own judgement about how many times oil can be reused. It depends on what's been fried and what kind of coating you used. If the coating is damp – like some batters – the oil will degrade more quickly. Air-drying the chicken after dredging it with flour makes the coating stick better, and less of it floats off into the oil.

Using gelatine to clarify the oil

This technique is widely attributed to J Kenji López-Alt, although in his *Serious Eats* article in 2019, he says he got the idea from a reader. He explains that gelatine, dissolved in water then stirred into warm oil, will clarify the oil in the same way that gelatine is used to clarify meat stocks. He writes that he was sceptical when he first heard about this technique, but he tried it and it works. I tried it, and yes, it does extend the life of used oil that's almost on its last legs.

For every litre (4⅓ cups) of used oil, you need 125ml (½ cup) of water and 1 teaspoon of powdered gelatine. Sprinkle the gelatine over the surface of the water, letting it absorb slowly before adding more. Leave to hydrate for a few minutes, then heat the water, either on the stove top or in the microwave. It should be just hot enough so the gelatine melts, but not boiling hot. Pour this into the oil, whisking constantly, then leave to cool completely. Refrigerate the oil.

The next day, pour off the now-clear oil into another container. At the bottom of the pot will be a lightly set gelatine disc full of the impurities it pulled out of the oil – scrape it out, then dispose of it in your rubbish bin.

When you first reuse this clarified oil, it will splatter quite a lot over the heat, but eventually the splattering will stop. This clarified oil should be fine for a couple more batches of chicken. I don't know if the clarifying with gelatine can be done a second time.

Disposing of the oil

I hope you know that you should never dispose of oil by pouring it down the sink – it will cause trouble down the line in the form of clogged drains. Instead, save the containers the oil came in. Pour used oil through a funnel into the containers, seal with the lid and throw it in the rubbish.

I've also used a Japanese product – a powder that, when stirred into used oil, turns it into a solid that you can throw in the bin. There are different brands of this 'oil solidifier', which you can buy online or at the Japanese equivalent of the pound shop or dollar store.

A WORD ON SERVING SIZES

I struggled with this because appetites can vary so greatly. I might eat six chicken wings with some rice and vegetables for dinner and be satisfied, but I know other people who can polish off 500g (1lb 2oz) of wings and still be hungry for more. How much each recipe serves also depends on what other dishes are prepared for the meal. If a kilo (2lb 4oz) of wings is served East or Southeast Asian family-style – with several other dishes to share, plus rice and vegetables – it could serve up to 8, but if it's the only dish on the table (apart from the starch and vegetables), it might be sufficient for only 2–4. In general – assuming the fried chicken is served with a couple of extra dishes to people with 'average' appetites, most of these recipes will feed 4–6, except where indicated.

KNOW YOUR CHICKEN PARTS

1. THE CHICKEN WING

The chicken wing is composed of three parts: the **drumette** (which looks like a miniature drumstick), the **middle joint**, which has two slender bones connected at the top and bottom, and the **tip**, which is mostly bone covered with skin (freeze them, then simmer with chicken bones to make a broth). The wing is easy to cut into separate parts: just cut between the joints.

WING TIP

DRUMETTE

MID-JOINT WING

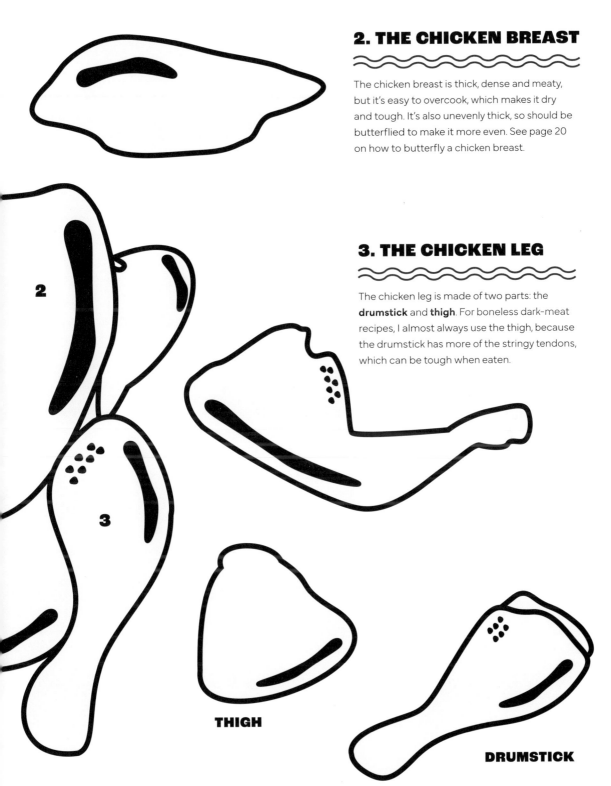

2. THE CHICKEN BREAST

The chicken breast is thick, dense and meaty, but it's easy to overcook, which makes it dry and tough. It's also unevenly thick, so should be butterflied to make it more even. See page 20 on how to butterfly a chicken breast.

3. THE CHICKEN LEG

The chicken leg is made of two parts: the **drumstick** and **thigh**. For boneless dark-meat recipes, I almost always use the thigh, because the drumstick has more of the stringy tendons, which can be tough when eaten.

THIGH

DRUMSTICK

FRIED CHICKEN

In this chapter, you will taste how incredibly varied fried chicken can be. Contrary to popular belief, it isn't necessarily crunchy. And even when it is crunchy, it's not always the same crunch. Some fried chicken has a hard, shattering crunch, while other versions have a crunchiness that is gentle and subtle.

Often, the difference in crunchiness is due to the coating. Chicken that is simply dredged in some type of flour (and there's far more choice beyond wheat flour, see page 12) will have a lighter crunch than chicken that's coated with batter before being fried. Chicken that's both battered and dredged in starch will be different from pieces that are dipped in starch, beaten egg and panko breadcrumbs. Sometimes I make a simple batter using just my basic coating mix (see page 162) and iced water, while other times the batter will have oil and vinegar – and these, too, yield different results.

Then there are the differences that come from what part of the chicken you're using, and how large the pieces are. A chicken breast will cook much more quickly than a thigh of the same weight. Because the batter and/or starch that coats the thighs spends a longer time in the hot oil, it will fry up crisper than if the same coating were used for breast meat. Bone-in parts of the bird have the hardest crunch of all, because they take the longest to fry.

I've grouped the recipes by their 'parts': wings, boneless dark meat, boneless white meat, and non-wing chicken with bones. I know that many people – including me – have strong preferences for their favourite parts, but I hope that you will try the recipes from the different categories.

WINGS

The wing is my favourite part of the chicken – well, after the back and innards. The wing is anatomically white meat, but because of the bones, it's not dry like the breast can be. The mid-joint has a double layer of delicious skin, and even the leaner drumette portion can be good, as long as it's not overcooked.

As I wrote earlier, chicken wings vary greatly in size. I've bought 1kg (2lb 4oz) bags that contained only 16 mid-joints or drumettes, and others that had 24 pieces. If you have a choice, buy the smaller wings. The exception is the recipes for stuffed wings, where you want larger mid-joint pieces, with the wing tip attached.

In some of these recipes, I slash the wings – both the mid-joint and drumette portions – to allow the marinade to penetrate. Place the mid-joint on the cutting board and cut two parallel slashes at a 45-degree angle to the length of the bone, then turn it over and repeat on the other side. For drumettes, I tend to give a single slash on the meatiest side, then another slash on the opposite side.

With other recipes that use only the mid-joint, I sometimes cut each one into two pieces, slicing between the bones so you have two long pieces, each with a single bone. This makes the wings much easier to eat, and also gives a larger proportion of surface area. I like to use this technique when the wings are cooked with a slightly dry coating, so more of it can cling to the meat.

MOM'S WINGS

4 peeled garlic cloves

4–6 thin slices of peeled ginger

140ml (generous ½ cup) soy sauce
   (all-purpose Kikkoman or your
   favourite brand)

20g (4 tsp) granulated sugar

75ml (5 tbsp) water

2–4 spring onions (scallions)

a few leaves of iceberg lettuce

For coating and frying the chicken

1kg (2lb 4oz) chicken wings – mid-joint
   and/or drumette portions

about 120g (4¼oz) potato flour or cornflour
   (cornstarch)

750ml (3¼ cups) cooking oil

It seems appropriate to start this book with the first fried chicken dish I remember eating, and also the first I learned to cook on my own. This is my mother's recipe, one that my brothers and I loved and asked her to make for us all the time when we were growing up. Later, when I was at university and teaching myself how to cook, I called my mother and asked for this recipe. I have changed it just slightly: she used cornflour (cornstarch) to coat the wings, but I prefer potato flour.

For the sauce, thinly slice the garlic cloves and julienne the ginger, then put them in a pan with the soy sauce, sugar and water. Do not cook yet; set aside.

Preheat the oven to 180°C/160°C fan/350°F/gas mark 4.

Dredge the wings in the potato flour or cornflour and shake off the excess. Lay the wings on a cooling rack placed over a tray and air-dry for 10 minutes.

Pour the cooking oil into a pan, preferably a medium wok, and place over a medium heat. Fry the chicken at 160°C (320°F) in four or five batches. Fry for 5–6 minutes, then drain on the rack placed over the tray. After frying the last batch, fry the wings again, this time at 170°C (340°F) for 1½ minutes.

Turn on the heat under the pan and bring the sauce to a simmer. Quickly coat the hot wings in the sauce, several at a time, and lay them on a foil-lined tray. After coating all the wings, use a pastry brush to brush them with any remaining sauce.

Place the tray in the oven and bake for 5 minutes. While the wings are baking, mince the spring onions and cut the iceberg lettuce into shreds.

Spread the shredded lettuce on a plate, add the chicken wings, then scatter with the spring onions.

TYPHOON SHELTER WINGS

Serves: 4–6

20g (¾oz) fermented black beans
   (see page 12)
15ml (1 tbsp) soy sauce
   (all-purpose Kikkoman or your
   favourite brand)
200g (7oz) peeled garlic cloves
6–12 red bird's-eye chillies
10–15 dried Tianjin chillies
120g (4¼oz) spring onions (scallions)
100g (3½oz) panko breadcrumbs
1½ tsp granulated sugar
5g (1 tsp) coarse salt flakes

For seasoning and frying the chicken
1kg (2lb 4oz) mid-joint chicken wings
coarse salt flakes, as necessary
about 120g (4¼oz) potato flour or
   sweet potato flour
870ml (3¾ cups) cooking oil

Note
*The garlic and breadcrumb mixture left over
after the wings are eaten can be kept in the
fridge for at least a week. It's delicious with rice
or congee, or sprinkled over scrambled eggs or
stir-fried vegetables.*

In Hong Kong, 'typhoon shelter' is a type of dish that developed on the boats that fished in local waters and is named after the coves that these boats would moor in at night and during inclement weather. Families that lived on the boats would cook for themselves – mostly with the seafood they caught, along with ingredients they purchased. Now, many of these boat people have moved onshore, but their style of cooking lives on in restaurants. Their most famous dish is probably Typhoon Shelter Crab: large, shell-on crab that's been cut into pieces, deep-fried, then stir-fried with loads of garlic, spring onions and chillies. At restaurants, diners choose the crab they want and indicate the spice level: for most people, medium is spicy enough. This style of cooking can be used for other ingredients, including prawns, fish, beancurd and chicken.

Cut the wings in half lengthways between the bones, then put the pieces in a bowl. Weigh the wings, then multiply the amount by 0.01 – this is the amount of salt you need. Sprinkle the salt over the wings, then mix well.

Briefly rinse the black beans, then put them in a small bowl and add 40ml (2 tbsp + 2 tsp) warm water and the soy sauce.

Roughly chop the garlic. Cut the bird's-eye chillies into thin rings, shaking out and discarding the seeds as you go. Briefly rinse the Tianjin chillies, then blot them dry. Cut them in half and shake out and discard the seeds, then slice them into thin rings. Cut the spring onions into 5cm (2in) lengths. Set aside.

Dredge the wings in the flour, then lay them on a cooling rack placed over a tray. Leave them to air-dry for at least 10 minutes, then coat them again.

Pour 750ml (3¼ cups) of the cooking oil into a pan, preferably a medium wok, and place over a medium heat. Fry the chicken at 160°C (320°F) in four or five batches. Fry for 3 minutes, then drain on the rack placed over the tray. After frying the last batch, fry the wings again, this time at 170°C (340°F) for 1 minute.

Place a large wok over a medium heat and add the remaining 120ml (½ cup) fresh oil. When the oil is at 100°C (212°F), add the panko, garlic, sugar and 5g (1 teaspoon) of salt. Stir almost constantly until the panko and garlic are pale golden. Mix in the black beans and their cooking liquid, both types of chillies and the spring onions and stir constantly for about 2 minutes, or until dry. Taste for seasonings and add more salt and sugar, if necessary. Add the wings and stir for about a further 3 minutes, or until the wings are hot.

Pile onto a platter and serve.

YANGNYEOM (SPICY & SWEET FRIED CHICKEN)

1kg (2lb 4oz) chicken wings – mid-joint
and/or drumette portions
coarse salt flakes, as necessary
3–5 peeled garlic cloves
1 tsp finely ground white pepper
100g (3½oz) coating mix made with
tapioca flour (see page 162)
about 40ml (2 tbsp + 2 tsp) iced water
20ml (4 tsp) coconut vinegar or distilled
white vinegar
770ml (3⅓ cups) cooking oil
about 120g (4¼oz) tapioca flour
toasted white sesame seeds

For the sauce

3–5 peeled garlic cloves
10g (⅓oz) thinly sliced peeled ginger
45g (1½oz) gochujang (Korean chilli paste)
30g (1oz) tomato ketchup
60g (2oz) golden syrup (or corn syrup)
20g (4 tsp) granulated sugar
15ml (1 tbsp) soy sauce
(all-purpose Kikkoman or your
favourite brand)
10ml (2 tsp) sesame oil
10–15g (⅓–½oz) gochugaru
(Korean chilli flakes)

If you've eaten KFC – Korean fried chicken – chances are high that the first version you tasted was the sweet and spicy Dakgangjeong or Yangnyeom. The two are very similar, but my Korean friends tell me that Dakgangjeong is sweeter and sticker, while Yangnyeom is spicier. I prefer the spicier version.

Prepare the ingredients for the sauce, but don't start to simmer it until just after you've completed the second frying. The sauce coats better when it and the wings are hot.

Weigh the wings, then multiply the amount by 0.01 – this is the amount of salt you need. Put the wings in a bowl and sprinkle the salt over them, then mix well. Mince the garlic cloves, then add them and the white pepper to the wings. Mix thoroughly, then set aside while preparing the sauce.

For the sauce, finely mince the garlic and ginger and put them in a saucepan. Add the gochujang, ketchup, syrup, sugar, soy sauce, sesame oil, gochugaru and 45ml (3 tablespoons) warm water, then mix well. Do not cook yet; set aside.

Put the coating mix in a bowl, add the iced water, vinegar and 20ml (4 teaspoons) of the cooking oil. Whisk to make a smooth batter that's slightly thick. Pour this over the wings and mix well. If the batter still seems too thick, drizzle in a little more iced water to create a batter that coats the wings lightly and evenly.

Dredge the battered wings in the tapioca flour, shake off the excess, then lay them on a cooling rack placed over a tray. Leave to air-dry for at least 10 minutes, then coat them again with tapioca flour.

Pour the remaining 750ml (3¼ cups) cooking oil into a pan, preferably a medium wok, set over a medium heat. Fry the chicken at 160°C (320°F) in four or five batches. Fry for 5–6 minutes, then drain on the rack placed over the tray. After frying the last batch, fry the wings again, this time at 170°C (340°F) for 1½ minutes.

Turn on the heat under the saucepan and simmer the sauce until a spatula leaves a track when you draw it across the bottom of the pan.

Put half of the freshly fried wings in a large bowl and drizzle half the sauce over them. Toss the wings in the bowl while gently stirring them, so they are lightly coated with the sauce. Sprinkle with sesame seeds, then put the wings on a serving plate. Repeat with the remaining wings and sauce. Serve with Korean Pickled White Radish (see page 166).

VIETNAMESE BUTTER WINGS

Serves: 4–6

1kg (2lb 4oz) chicken wings – mid-joint and/or drumette portions
coarse salt flakes, as necessary
about 130g (4½oz) coating mix, preferably made with potato or sweet potato flour (see page 162)
about 120g (4¼oz) potato flour or sweet potato flour
770ml (3⅓ cups) cooking oil

For the marinade and seasonings
90ml (6 tbsp) fish sauce
40ml (2 tbsp + 2 tsp) fresh lime juice
10ml (2 tsp) rice vinegar
10g (2 tsp) granulated sugar
4–6 peeled garlic cloves
20g (¾oz) fresh lemongrass (the lower 8cm/3¼in of the stalk)
2–4 red bird's-eye chillies
1 red banana chilli
60g (2oz) spring onions (scallions)
½ tsp coarse salt flakes, or to taste
90g (3oz) unsalted butter

I've never eaten these wings in Vietnam, although it is possible that I have been searching in the wrong places. However, I have seen butter chicken wings on the menu of almost every Vietnamese restaurant I have visited in the USA, Hong Kong and other countries, leaving me to wonder if it was something created by the Vietnamese diaspora. The addition of butter to a Vietnamese dish makes sense when you think of the strong French influence on the cuisine.

Slash the mid-joint wings twice on each side, and the drumette portions once on each side, then put the pieces in a bowl. Weigh the wings, then multiply the amount by 0.01 – this is the amount of salt you need. Sprinkle the salt over the wings and mix well, then stir in the fish sauce, lime juice, rice vinegar and sugar. Marinate at room temperature for 1–3 hours (or longer in the fridge), mixing occasionally.

Thinly slice the garlic cloves. Use the flat side of a metal meat mallet to bash the entire lower 8cm (3¼in) of each lemongrass stalk to flatten it. Slice the lemongrass as thinly as possible. Slice the bird's-eye chillies into thin rings, shaking out and discarding the seeds as you go. Halve the banana chilli lengthways, then slice it on the diagonal. Mince the spring onions. Set aside.

Sprinkle the coating mix over the wings and mix well. Adjust the consistency as necessary by adding some iced water to create a batter that coats the wings lightly and evenly.

Dredge the battered wings in the potato or sweet potato flour, shake off the excess, then lay them on a cooling rack placed over a tray. Leave them to air-dry for at least 10 minutes.

Pour 750ml (3¼ cups) of the cooking oil into a pan, preferably a medium wok, set over a medium heat. Fry the chicken at 160°C (320°F) in four or five batches. Fry for 5–6 minutes, then drain on the rack placed over the tray. After frying the last batch, fry the wings again, this time at 170°C (340°F) for 1½ minutes.

Pour the remaining 20ml (4 teaspoons) cooking oil into a large wok set over a medium–high heat. When the oil is hot, add the garlic, lemongrass and both types of chillies. Stir-fry for about 30 seconds or until fragrant. Add the spring onions and salt and mix briefly. Taste for seasonings and adjust, if necessary.

Add the butter to the wok and, when it's about half melted, add the wings. Mix until the wings are lightly coated with the butter and other ingredients. Pile onto a plate and serve.

SAMBAL GORENG WINGS

〜〜〜〜〜〜〜〜〜〜〜〜〜〜〜〜〜〜〜〜〜 **Serves: 4–6**

1kg (2lb 4oz) chicken wings – mid-joint and/or drumette portions
coarse salt flakes, as necessary
100g (3½oz) coating mix, preferably made with potato flour or sweet potato flour (see page 162)
about 40ml (2 tbsp + 2 tsp) iced water
20ml (4 tsp) coconut vinegar or distilled white vinegar
770ml (3⅓ cups) cooking oil
about 120g (4¼oz) potato flour or sweet potato flour
180g (6¼oz) sambal goreng (see below)
60ml (¼ cup) canned coconut milk
about 15g (½oz) unsweetened shredded coconut, toasted

For the sambal goreng
50g (1¾oz) peeled garlic cloves
300g (10½oz) peeled shallots
4 candlenuts or macadamia nuts (see note)
10g (⅓oz) Tianjin chillies – use as needed
120g (½ cup) tamarind paste
100g (3½oz) tomato purée (paste)
about 15g (1 tbsp) coarse salt flakes
about 20g (4 tsp) granulated sugar
90ml (6 tbsp) cooking oil

Note
Candlenuts aren't easy to find, even in shops that specialize in Indonesian ingredients. I buy them when I see them and store them in the freezer. If I run out, I substitute them with macadamia nuts. They're not the same, but macadamias also have a high fat content. This amount of Tianjin chillies makes a sambal that's quite spicy; you can use less, if you want.

For this dish, you need to make the sambal goreng – an Indonesian fried chilli paste – at least one day in advance so the flavours have time to blend. Once it's ready, preparing the wings is easy. This amount of sambal goreng is enough for 2½ batches of wings. If the surface of the sambal is covered in a layer of oil and kept in an airtight jar, it keeps for up to two months in the fridge.

To make the sambal goreng, roughly chop the garlic, shallots and nuts and put them in a blender (preferably a high-speed one). Briefly rinse the dried chillies, then dry them, tear them in half and shake out and discard the seeds. Weigh out 5g (1 teaspoon) of the chillies (or less, if you want it less spicy) and add them to the blender along with the tamarind paste.

Blend the ingredients to a rough purée, adding some of the tomato purée, if necessary – with some blenders if there's too much liquid, the solid ingredients just swirl around on the blades without being puréed. You need just enough liquid so the blades 'catch' the solid ingredients and chop them. When the ingredients are a rough purée, mix in the remaining tomato purée and the salt and sugar.

Scrape the mixture into a wok, add the oil and place over a medium heat. Cook until sizzling, stirring frequently. Reduce the heat to low, then cook for about 20 minutes, or until thick and glossy. Stir often and reduce the heat as the mixture starts to thicken. It's ready when the oil starts to seep out around the edges of the purée. Cool the sambal, then put into a clean jar and allow to cool. If necessary, add more oil so it coats the surface of the sambal. Cover the jar and refrigerate for at least a day.

Slash the mid-joint wings twice on each side, and the drumette portions once on each side, then put them in a bowl. Weigh the wings, then multiply the amount by 0.015 – this is the amount of salt you need. Sprinkle the salt over the wings, mix well and leave for at least 15 minutes.

Put the coating mix in a bowl and add the iced water, vinegar and 20ml (4 teaspoons) of the cooking oil. Whisk to make a smooth, thick batter. Pour this over the wings and mix well. If the mixture seems too thick, drizzle in a little more iced water to create a batter that coats the chicken lightly and evenly.

Dredge the battered wings in the potato or sweet potato flour. Lay them on a cooling rack placed over a tray and leave them to air-dry for at least 10 minutes.

Pour the remaining 750ml (3¼ cups) cooking oil into a pan, preferably a medium wok, set over a medium heat. Fry the chicken at 160°C (320°F) in four or five

batches. Fry for 5–6 minutes, then drain on the rack placed over the tray. After frying the last batch, fry the wings again, this time at 170°C (340°F) for 1½ minutes.

Put 180g (6¼oz) of sambal goreng into a large wok placed over a medium heat. Add the coconut milk and heat until simmering, stirring often. Add all the wings to the wok and stir to coat them with the sambal mixture. Stir constantly over a very low heat until the sambal dries out slightly – it will be matte, not glossy.

Scatter the toasted coconut shreds over the wings, then serve.

SALT & PEPPER WINGS

~~~~~~ **Serves: 4–6**

8–10 red bird's-eye chillies
250g (9oz) red and green banana chillies
40g (1½oz) peeled garlic cloves
60g (2oz) spring onions (scallions)
10g (2 tsp) coarse salt flakes
½ tsp granulated sugar
1½ tsp medium-grind black pepper
½ tsp medium-grind white pepper
Thai limes, to serve

For seasoning and frying the chicken
1kg (2lb 4oz) mid-joint chicken wings
coarse salt flakes, as necessary
100g (3½oz) coating mix (see page 162)
¾ tsp garlic powder
about 60ml (¼ cup) iced water
800ml (3½ cups) cooking oil

Salt and pepper squid is a popular dish in many parts of East and Southeast Asia. The squid rings and tentacles are coated in batter, deep-fried, then mixed with salt, pepper, garlic and chillies. The same cooking method works well with chicken wings.

For the best flavour, freshly grind the black and white peppercorns.

Cut the wings in half lengthways between the bones, then put the pieces in a bowl. Weigh the wings, then multiply the amount by 0.01 – this is the amount of salt you need. Sprinkle the salt over the wings, then mix well.

Cut the bird's-eye chillies into thin rings, shaking out and discarding the seeds as you go. Halve the banana chillies lengthways, then slice them on the diagonal. Slice the garlic cloves and mince the spring onions. Set aside.

Put the coating mix in a bowl and whisk in the garlic powder. Add the iced water and 20ml (4 teaspoons) of the cooking oil and whisk until smooth to make a slightly thick batter. Pour this over the wings and mix. If necessary, adjust the consistency by adding more iced water to create a batter that coats the wings lightly and evenly.

Pour 750ml (3¼ cups) of the cooking oil into a pan, preferably a medium wok, set over a medium heat. Fry the chicken at 160°C (320°F) in four or five batches. Fry for 3 minutes, then drain on a cooling rack placed over a tray. After frying the last batch, fry the wings again, this time at 170°C (340°F) for 1 minute.

Pour the remaining 30ml (2 tablespoons) of fresh oil into a large wok placed over a medium–high heat. Swirl the wok to coat it with the oil, and when it's hot, add the garlic and both types of chillies and stir-fry until the garlic just starts to take on a little colour. Mix in the spring onions, the 10g (2 tsp) of salt, the sugar and both types of pepper and stir-fry until the spring onions start to wilt. Taste for seasonings and add more sugar, salt and/or black and white pepper, if necessary.

Add the wings and stir-fry for about 2 minutes until hot, then pile the ingredients onto a platter and serve with Thai limes, cut as directed on page 15.

SHRIMP PASTE WINGS

Serves: 4–6

1kg (2lb 4oz) chicken wings – mid-joint and/or drumette portions
3–5 peeled garlic cloves
50g (1¾oz) fermented shrimp paste
30g (2 tbsp) granulated sugar
25ml (5 tsp) fish sauce
20ml (4 tsp) rice wine
1 tsp finely ground white pepper
20ml (4 tsp) sesame oil
2 tsp gochugaru (Korean chilli flakes)
90g (3oz) coating mix, preferably using potato or sweet potato flour (see page 162)
about 30ml (2 tbsp) iced water
120g (4¼oz) potato or sweet potato flour, for dredging
750ml (3¼ cups) cooking oil

Fermented shrimp paste (also called prawn paste) has a very strong odour, but its bark is far worse than its bite. It is too potent to consume on its own; instead, the paste is mixed with other ingredients, and is used raw or cooked. I've eaten versions of chicken with shrimp paste in Hong Kong, Malaysia and Singapore, and all have been delicious. The dish isn't always made with wings: one of the very best versions I ate was at a high-end Chinese restaurant in Hong Kong, where they used small pieces of boneless meat. My recipe is more like the dish that's found at hawker centres in Malaysia and Singapore. It uses the soft shrimp paste sold in jars, instead of the hard, brick-like type that needs to be crumbled and toasted. It's a good idea to wear a disposable glove when mixing the wings, or else the smell of the shrimp paste will linger on your hands.

If you want to make this dish as it's often done in Malaysia and Singapore, use whole wings – with the drumette, mid-joint and wing tip – and cook them for 7 minutes for the first frying, and 2 minutes for the second. The whole wing is harder to eat, though, so I use the drumette and mid-joint separated into different parts.

Slash the mid-joint wings twice on each side, and the drumette portions once on each side, then put them in a bowl.

Mince the garlic cloves, then mix them with the shrimp paste, sugar, fish sauce, rice wine, white pepper, sesame oil and gochugaru. Pour this over the wings and mix well. Cover the bowl tightly (to contain the smell), then marinate at room temperature for 2–3 hours (or up to 24 hours in the fridge), mixing occasionally.

Add the coating mix and the iced water to the bowl of wings and mix well to create a batter that coats the pieces lightly and evenly. If necessary, adjust the consistency by mixing in more iced water.

Dredge the battered wings in the potato or sweet potato flour and lay them on a rack placed over a tray.

Pour the cooking oil into a pan, preferably a medium wok, set over a medium heat. Fry the chicken at 160°C (320°F) in four or five batches. Fry for 5–6 minutes, then drain on the rack placed over the tray. After frying the last batch, fry the wings again, this time at 170°C (340°F) for 1½ minutes.

Serve the wings hot, warm or at room temperature.

COLA WINGS

20g (¾oz) thinly sliced peeled ginger
2–3 peeled garlic cloves
4–6 red bird's-eye chillies
10ml (2 tsp) fish sauce
5g (1 tsp) granulated sugar
10ml (2 tsp) fresh lime juice
2 spring onions (scallions)
400ml (1¾ cups) cola
20g (4 tsp) oyster sauce

For seasoning and frying the chicken
1kg (2lb 4oz) chicken wings – mid-joint
   and/or drumette portions
coarse salt flakes, as necessary
100g (3½oz) coating mix (see page 162)
about 70ml (2¼fl oz) iced water
750ml (3¼ cups) cooking oil

This Vietnamese recipe was given to me by a friend, Elizabeth Chu, who was born in Saigon and now runs the family restaurant business in Hong Kong, ZS Hospitality. She says this easy recipe comes from her aunt who lives in Vietnam. You can use a generic brand of cola, but don't use a diet or low-cal version, because the terrible taste of the artificial sugars will be enhanced.

Slash the mid-joint wings twice on each side, and the drumette portions once on each side, then put them in a bowl. Weigh the wings, then multiply the amount by 0.01 – this is the amount of salt you need. Sprinkle the salt over the wings and mix well.

For the sauce, mince the ginger and slice the garlic cloves. Cut the chillies into thin rings, shaking out and discarding the seeds as you go. Set aside. In a separate bowl, mix the fish sauce with the sugar and lime juice. Mince the spring onions. Set aside.

Pour the cola into a bowl and mix in the oyster sauce, ginger, garlic and chillies. Set aside.

Add the coating mix and the iced water to the bowl of wings and mix well to create a batter that coats the pieces lightly and evenly. If necessary, adjust the consistency by mixing in more iced water.

Pour the cooking oil into a pan, preferably a medium wok, set over a medium heat. Fry the chicken at 160°C (320°F) in four or five batches. Fry for 5–6 minutes, then drain on a rack placed over a tray. After frying the last batch, fry the wings again, this time at 170°C (340°F) for 1½ minutes.

Pour the cola mixture into a large wok and bring to the boil over a high heat. Stir often and reduce the mixture until the sauce leaves a thick track when you draw a spatula across the bottom of the pan.

Stir in the fish sauce mixture and simmer for 1 minute, then add the wings. Mix to coat the wings with the sauce, then stir over a medium heat until the glaze is sizzling, thick and sticky. The wings will start to brown in spots, and the ginger, garlic and chillies will stick to the glaze.

Scatter the spring onions over the wings and mix well, then pile the ingredients onto a platter to serve.

KOREAN FRIED WINGS WITH WILTED SPRING ONION SALAD

Serves: 4–6

1kg (2lb 4oz) chicken wings – mid-joint and/or drumette portions
coarse salt flakes, as necessary
1 tsp finely ground white pepper
about 120g (4¼oz) potato or sweet potato flour
750ml (3¼ cups) cooking oil

For the spring onion salad
200g (7oz) spring onions (scallions)
30ml (2 tbsp) soy sauce (all-purpose Kikkoman or your favourite brand)
10–15g (2 tsp–1 tbsp) granulated sugar
½ tsp coarse salt flakes
30ml (2 tbsp) sesame oil
2 tsp gochugaru (Korean chilli flakes)
2 tsp toasted sesame seeds, plus extra for sprinkling

This is another version of KFC, and one of my favourites. The thought of shredding 200g (7oz) of spring onions (scallions) seems tedious, but it goes more quickly if you use a spring onion shredder (see page 17). When I'm using a lot of spring onions in a dish, I usually soak them in a bowl of iced water. This makes them curl (if they're shredded), and also makes them taste milder. If you like, you can use 100g (3½oz) of shredded spring onions and 100g (3½oz) of red leaf lettuce torn into bite-sized pieces.

This version of KFC has a softer coating than the one for Yangnyeom on page 35 because the spring onion salad is lighter and more delicate than the spicy glaze.

Weigh the wings, then multiply the amount by 0.015 – this is the amount of salt you need. Sprinkle the salt and white pepper over the wings and mix well.

Shred the spring onions, then cut them into 6cm (2½in) lengths. Put the spring onions in a bowl of iced water and leave to soak for about 15 minutes.

Mix the soy sauce with the sugar, salt, 20ml (4 teaspoons) of the sesame oil, the gochugaru and 2 teaspoons of sesame seeds and stir until the sugar dissolves. Set aside.

Dredge the wings in the potato or sweet potato flour, shake off the excess, then lay them on a cooling rack placed over a tray. Leave for about 10 minutes, then dredge again.

Pour the cooking oil into a pan, preferably a medium wok, set over a medium heat. Fry the chicken at 160°C (320°F) in four or five batches. Fry for 5–6 minutes, then drain on the rack placed over the tray. After frying the last batch, fry the wings again, this time at 170°C (340°F) for 1½ minutes.

Drain the spring onions, then spin them dry in a salad spinner. If you don't have a salad spinner, roll the spring onions loosely but securely in a dry dish towel. Holding both ends of the dish towel 'roll', spin it and shake it up and down to remove the excess moisture.

Put the spring onions in a bowl and drizzle with the remaining 10ml (2 teaspoons) of sesame oil. Mix with your hands to lightly coat the spring onions. Pour the soy dressing over the spring onions and mix quickly.

Place the wings on a serving plate and pile the salad over the wings. Sprinkle with more sesame seeds before serving.

WINGS WITH THAI RED CURRY PASTE & MAKRUT LIME LEAVES

Serves: 4–6

1kg (2lb 4oz) chicken wings – mid-joint
   and/or drumette portions
coarse salt flakes, as necessary
16–20 pairs of makrut lime leaves
50g (1¾oz) Thai red curry paste
30ml (2 tbsp) soy sauce
   (all-purpose Kikkoman or your
   favourite brand)
1½ tsp granulated sugar
40ml (2 tbsp + 2 tsp) canned
   coconut milk
1 tsp finely ground white pepper
100g (3½oz) coating mix (see page 162)
about 40ml (2 tbsp + 2 tsp) iced water
750ml (3¼ cups) cooking oil

If you're the DIY type, you'll probably insist on making your own red curry paste. I don't know if it's worth it for this recipe, though, and I am perfectly happy using commercial brands. Buy small packs of curry paste produced in Thailand, and store in the fridge or freezer.

Slash the mid-joint wings twice on each side, and the drumette portions once on each side, then put the pieces in a bowl. Weigh the wings, then multiply the amount by 0.01 – this is the amount of salt you need. Sprinkle the salt over the wings and mix well.

Separate the pairs of lime leaves into individual leaves. Tear out or cut out the tough midrib of 8–10 pairs of the lime leaves, then stack them and slice them as thinly as possible. Leave the remaining lime leaves whole – lay them on a dish towel and blot them dry to remove any excess moisture.

Mix the curry paste with the soy sauce, sugar, coconut milk, pepper and the shredded lime leaves. Add this to the wings and mix well, then marinate at room temperature for 1–3 hours.

Add the coating mix and the iced water to the bowl of wings and mix well to create a batter that coats the pieces lightly and evenly. If necessary, adjust the consistency by mixing in more iced water.

Pour the cooking oil into a pan, preferably a medium wok, set over a medium heat. Add the whole lime leaves and fry at 150–160°C (300–320°F) until the leaves curl and darken slightly. Drain on paper towels.

Fry the chicken at 160°C (320°F) in four or five batches. Fry for 5–6 minutes, then drain on a rack placed over a tray. After frying the last batch, fry the wings again, this time at 170°C (340°F) for 1½ minutes.

Pile the wings onto a platter and garnish with the fried lime leaves.

WINGS WITH PONZU & YUZU DRESSING

Serves: 4–6

1kg (2lb 4oz) chicken wings – preferably
   mid-joint with the wing tip
coarse salt flakes, as necessary
1 tsp finely ground white pepper
about 120g (4¼oz) potato or sweet
   potato flour
750ml (3¼ cups) cooking oil
toasted sesame seeds

For the dressing
2–3 peeled garlic cloves
100ml (scant ½ cup) soy sauce
   (all-purpose Kikkoman or your
   favourite brand)
100ml (scant ½ cup) ponzu
40ml (2 tbsp + 2 tsp) sake
30g (2 tbsp) granulated sugar
25ml (5 tsp) yuzu juice

This recipe makes wings similar to the type you find at izakaya and kushikatsu (fried skewers) restaurants. After being fried, the wings are dipped into a sauce, which, naturally enough, slightly softens the crispness. The wings are at their absolute best eaten within 10 minutes of being fried and dipped but are delicious even when the crispness has entirely faded. Izakaya frequently serve the mid-joint portion with the wing tip attached, so use them, if possible. Bottled ponzu is fairly easy to find, but bottled yuzu might be more difficult – look for it at shops specializing in Japanese ingredients. If you can't find yuzu juice, use equal parts of fresh orange, lemon and lime juice to total 25ml (5 teaspoons).

Weigh the wings, then multiply the amount by 0.01 – this is the amount of salt you need. Sprinkle the salt and pepper over the wings, then mix well.

For the dressing, grate the garlic cloves, preferably on a ceramic oroshigane (see page 17). Put the grated garlic into a small saucepan and add the soy sauce, ponzu, sake and sugar; do not cook yet, set aside. Pour the yuzu juice into a small bowl and place it near the stove top.

Dredge the wings in the potato or sweet potato flour to coat them lightly, then shake off the excess and lay the pieces on a cooling rack placed over a tray. Leave them to air-dry for at least 10 minutes, then dredge them a second time, again shaking off the excess.

Pour the cooking oil into a pan, preferably a medium wok, set over a medium heat. Fry the chicken at 160°C (320°F) in four or five batches. Fry for 5–6 minutes, then drain on the rack placed over the tray. After frying the last batch, fry the wings again, this time at 170°C (340°F) for 1½ minutes.

While the wings are frying the second time, turn on the heat under the saucepan and heat the sauce to boiling. Turn off the heat and stir in the yuzu juice.

Pour half of the sauce into a large bowl and add half the wings. Toss the wings in the bowl while gently stirring them so they are lightly coated with the sauce, then pile them on a serving plate. Repeat with the remaining sauce and wings. Sprinkle sesame seeds over the wings and serve.

SALTED EGG YOLK WINGS

Serves: 4–6

8 salted duck eggs (see note)
20ml (4 tsp) rice wine
5g (1 tsp) coarse salt flakes
½ tsp granulated sugar
½ tsp finely ground white pepper
6 x 10cm (4in) stalks of fresh curry leaves
4 red bird's-eye chillies
40g (1½oz) unsalted butter

For seasoning and frying the chicken
1kg (2lb 4oz) mid-joint chicken wings
coarse salt flakes, as necessary
100g (3½oz) coating mix (see page 162)
about 70ml (4½ tbsp) iced water
about 120g (4¼oz) potato, sweet potato or
    tapioca flour
750ml (3¼ cups) cooking oil

Note
*Some salted duck eggs are covered with an
ash layer that needs to be removed before the
eggs are cooked. Use a blunt knife to scrape
away the ash, then rinse the egg thoroughly
before proceeding with the recipe.*

These wings will satisfy anyone who likes salted egg yolks. Usually shops sell uncooked salted eggs, which are made from duck eggs because these have a richer yolk than chicken eggs. In parts of South-east Asia, the eggs are sold already cooked, and they're usually dyed or marked somehow, so they can't be mistaken for plain, un-salted eggs. If you have the cooked eggs, there's no need to steam them – discard the shell and egg white and continue with the rest of the recipe. If you buy just the uncooked salted egg yolks (sold out of the shell) skip the first sentence of the second step of the instructions.

Cut the wings in half lengthways between the bones, then put the pieces in a bowl. Weigh the wings, then multiply the amount by 0.005 – this is the amount of salt you need. Sprinkle the salt over the wings and mix well.

If using whole uncooked salted eggs, crack them open and discard the whites. Put the yolks on a small plate and cover with a paper towel. Put the plate on a low metal rack placed in a wok with about 1.5cm (⅝in) of water. Bring the water to the boil, cover the wok with the lid and steam the egg yolks for 10 minutes.

Put the yolks in a bowl, then use the tines of a fork to mash them while they are warm until they are very smooth. Mix in the rice wine, salt, sugar and white pepper. Set aside.

Remove the leaves from the curry leaf stalks. Slice the chillies into thin rings, shaking out and discarding the seeds as you go. Set aside.

Add the coating mix and the iced water to the bowl of wings and mix well to create a batter that coats the pieces lightly and evenly. If necessary, adjust the consistency by mixing in more iced water.

Dredge the battered wings in the flour and lay the pieces on a cooling rack.

Pour the cooking oil into a pan, preferably a medium wok, set over a medium heat. Fry the wings at 160°C (320°F) in four or five batches. Fry for 3 minutes, then drain on a cooling rack placed over a tray. After frying the last batch, fry the wings again, this time at 170°C (340°F) for 1 minute.

Put the butter in a large wok and melt it over a low heat. Add the curry leaves and chillies and cook until sizzling.

Stir in the egg yolk mixture, then add the wings. Stir constantly over a medium–low heat until the egg yolk mixture coats the wings and they are hot and sizzling. Pile onto a plate, then serve.

VIETNAMESE HONEY-MUSTARD GARLIC WINGS

30g (1oz) peeled garlic cloves
20g (¾oz) unsalted butter
2 tsp Tianjin chilli powder, or to taste
10g (⅓oz) grainy mustard
100g (3½oz) honey
20ml (4 tsp) fish sauce
30ml (2 tbsp) fresh lime juice

For seasoning and frying the chicken
1kg (2lb 4oz) chicken wings – mid-joint
    and/or drumette portions
coarse salt flakes, as necessary
2 tsp finely ground white pepper
100g (3½oz) coating mix (see page 162)
about 70ml (4½ tbsp) iced water
about 120g (4¼oz) potato, sweet potato or
    tapioca flour
750ml (3¼ cups) cooking oil

Here's another easy and delicious recipe from Elizabeth Chu, who, again, attributes it to her aunt. I adapted it slightly, using grainy mustard instead of the yellow mustard called for in the original recipe, and I slightly increased the chilli to balance the sweetness.

Slash the mid-joint wings twice on each side, and the drumette portions once on each side and put them in a bowl. Weigh the wings, then multiply the amount by 0.01 – this is the amount of salt you need. Sprinkle the salt and white pepper over the wings and mix well.

Add the coating mix and the iced water to the wings and mix well to create a batter that coats the pieces lightly and evenly. If necessary, adjust the consistency by mixing in more iced water. Dredge the wings in the potato, sweet potato or tapioca flour and lay them on a cooling rack placed over a tray.

Pour the cooking oil into a pan, preferably a medium wok, set over a medium heat. Fry the chicken at 160°C (320°F) in four or five batches. Fry for 5–6 minutes, then drain on a cooling rack placed over a tray. After frying the last batch, fry the wings again, this time at 170°C (340°F) for 1½ minutes.

Mince the garlic. Put the butter in a large wok over a low heat. When the butter melts and starts to sizzle, add the garlic and cook for about 30 seconds. Add the chilli powder, mustard, honey and fish sauce and cook over a medium–high heat until sizzling. Stir constantly until the sauce leaves a thick track when you draw a spatula across the bottom of the pan.

Stir in the lime juice, then simmer again. Add the wings, then turn off the heat and mix until the wings are lightly coated. Turn the heat to medium–low and continue to mix the wings until they start to brown in spots. Pile the wings onto a plate and serve.

THAI GARLIC WINGS

16 peeled garlic cloves

6 spring onions (scallions)

½ tsp granulated sugar

½ tsp soy sauce
(all-purpose Kikkoman or your
favourite brand)

½ tsp Thai chilli flakes

Thai limes, to serve

For seasoning, coating and frying the chicken

1kg (2lb 4oz) chicken wings – mid-joint
and/or drumette portions

2 red bird's-eye chillies

2–3 peeled garlic cloves

15g (½oz) coriander (cilantro) roots
with about 2.5cm (1in) of the stem
(see page 14)

80ml (⅓ cup) fish sauce

20g (4 tsp) granulated sugar

20ml (4 tsp) fresh lime juice

1 tsp finely ground white pepper

about 100g (3½oz) coating mix
(see page 162)

770ml (3⅓ cups) cooking oil

I learned how to make these wings years ago from a Thai friend and they were so popular with my other friends that if I invited them to dinner, they would invariably request that I make these. I often made a double batch so they would have leftovers to take home.

Slash the mid-joint wings twice on each side, and the drumette portions once on each side, then put them in a bowl.

Slice the bird's eye chillies into thin rings, squeezing out and discarding the seeds as you go. Roughly chop the garlic and coriander roots, then put them in a mortar along with the chillies. Pound to a rough paste, then transfer to a bowl.

Add the fish sauce, sugar, lime juice and pepper to the paste and mix well, then pour this over the wings. Mix well, then marinate at room temperature for 2–3 hours, or longer in the fridge.

Sprinkle the coating mix over the wings and mix until they are thoroughly coated, without any damp spots.

Pour 750ml (3¼ cups) of the cooking oil into a pan, preferably a medium wok, set over a medium heat. Fry the chicken at 160°C (320°F) in four or five batches. Fry for 5–6 minutes, then drain on a cooling rack placed over a tray. After frying the last batch, fry the wings again, this time at 170°C (340°F) for 1½ minutes.

Cool the oil slightly. Roughly chop the garlic and mince the spring onions. Put the garlic in the oil and fry at 150°C (300°F) until very pale golden, then scoop it out of the wok with a shallow mesh sieve (strainer). Drain briefly.

Pour the remaining 20ml (4 teaspoons) of oil into a large wok over a low heat. Add the fried garlic and the sugar and soy sauce. Stir constantly until the garlic darkens slightly, then mix in the spring onions and Thai chilli flakes. Add the wings and mix until the ingredients are combined.

Put the wings on a platter and serve with Thai limes, cut as directed on page 15.

GARLIC & BLACK PEPPER WINGS

Serves: 4–6

90g (3oz) Chinese celery (see page 14)
90g (3oz) spring onions (scallions)
80g (2¾oz) peeled garlic cloves
240g (8½oz) peeled onion
15g (½oz) thinly sliced peeled ginger
8–12 dried Tianjin chillies
4–8 red bird's-eye chillies
30ml (2 tbsp) soy sauce
  (all-purpose Kikkoman or your
  favourite brand)
20ml (4 tsp) rice wine
10g (2 tsp) granulated sugar
1½–2 tsp freshly ground black pepper
5g (1 tsp) coarse salt flakes, or to taste

For seasoning and frying the chicken

1kg (2lb 4oz) mid-joint chicken wings
coarse salt flakes, as necessary
100g (3½oz) coating mix (see page 162)
about 70ml (4½ tbsp) iced water
about 120g (4¼oz) potato, sweet potato or
  tapioca flour
800ml (3½ cups) cooking oil

Everyone has their own opinion about how much pepper is too much, so I erred on the side of caution with this dish – feel free to adjust the pepper to your own tastes. Actually, though, the heat level of pepper doesn't depend solely on the amount you use – it also depends on the variety and where it's grown. Some types of black pepper are more powerful than others, and some have a more complex flavour that isn't just a peppery hotness. For this dish it's better to use freshly ground black pepper, instead of the pre-ground stuff.

Cut the wings in half lengthways between the bones, then put the pieces in a bowl. Weigh the wings, then multiply the amount by 0.01 – this is the amount of salt you need. Sprinkle the salt over the wings and mix well.

Remove the leaves from the celery stalks and set them aside for the garnish. Tear the celery stalks into 5cm (2in) lengths. Cut the spring onions into 2.5cm (1in) lengths. Slice the garlic cloves, cut the onion into 1cm (½in) pieces and julienne the ginger. Briefly rinse the Tianjin chillies and blot them dry, then tear them into 2–3 pieces (depending on the size), shaking out and discarding the seeds. Cut the bird's-eye chillies into thin rings, shaking out and discarding the seeds as you go.

Pour the soy sauce into a bowl then mix in the rice wine, sugar and 30ml (2 tablespoons) water. Put the pepper and salt into a small dish. Set aside.

Add the coating mix and the iced water to the bowl of wings and mix well to create a batter that coats the pieces lightly and evenly. If necessary, adjust the consistency by mixing in more iced water. Dredge the wings in the potato, sweet potato or tapioca flour and lay them on a cooling rack placed over a tray.

Pour 750ml (3¼ cups) of the cooking oil into a pan, preferably a medium wok, set over a medium heat. Fry the chicken at 160°C (320°F) in four or five batches. Fry for 3 minutes, then drain on a rack placed over a tray. After frying the last batch, fry the wings again, this time at 170°C (340°F) for 1 minute.

Pour 30ml (2 tablespoons) of the cooking oil into a large wok, set over a high heat. When the oil is hot, add the Chinese celery and spring onions. Stir-fry briefly until the spring onions turn bright green, then remove the ingredients from the wok.

Reduce the heat to medium–low and add the remaining 20ml (4 teaspoons) of cooking oil. Add the garlic and cook until it starts to colour, stirring often. Increase the heat to high, add the onion and ginger and stir-fry until the onion starts to soften. Mix in the dried and fresh chillies. Stir in the soy sauce mixture and bring to the boil.

Add the wings and mix constantly over a high heat until the wings are lightly coated with the sauce, and not too wet. Add the Chinese celery and spring onions. Sprinkle the pepper and salt around the ingredients (not over them) and mix in. Taste for seasonings and add more salt and pepper, if necessary. Pile the ingredients onto a platter, garnish with the reserved celery leaves and serve.

SRIRACHA WINGS

Serves: 4–6

1kg (2lb 4oz) chicken wings – mid-joint and/or drumette portions
coarse salt flakes, as necessary
2 tsp finely ground white pepper
100g (3½oz) coating mix (see page 162)
about 70ml (4½ tbsp) iced water, or as necessary
about 120g (4¼oz) potato, sweet potato or tapioca flour
750ml (3¼ cups) cooking oil

For the sauce
120g (4¼oz) sriracha
60g (2oz) tomato purée (paste)
½ tsp finely ground white pepper
40g (2 tbsp + 2 tsp) granulated sugar
½ tsp Tianjin chilli powder, or to taste (optional)
10ml (2 tsp) white vinegar
2 spring onions (scallions)

Sriracha is just one of the hundreds of nam priks – Thai sauces served as condiments to spice up a dish. It was popularized in the United States of America by a Vietnamese producer in California. In Thailand, you won't see a bottle of sriracha on the table of every other noodle shop in the country, which seems to be the case in the USA. I'm not naming a specific brand here, because what you can find depends on where you live. Different brands have different amounts of acidity and heat, so you might need to adjust the seasonings slightly to balance the flavours. If your preferred brand is very hot or vinegary, add a little more sugar, or, if you like it spicier, mix in more chilli powder.

I learned this recipe from a friend, Tass, who is the best Thai home cook I know.

Slash the mid-joint wings twice on each side, and the drumette portions once on each side, then put them in a bowl. Weigh the wings, then multiply the amount by 0.015 – this is the amount of salt you need. Sprinkle the salt and pepper over the wings and mix well.

For the sauce, mix the sriracha with the tomato purée, pepper, sugar, chilli powder and 60ml (¼ cup) water in a bowl or liquid measuring cup; set aside. Put the vinegar in a small bowl and place it by the stove top. Mince the spring onions. Set aside.

Add the coating mix and the iced water to the bowl of wings and mix well to create a batter that coats the pieces lightly and evenly. If necessary, adjust the consistency by mixing in more iced water.

Dredge the battered wings in the flour, shake off the excess, then lay them on a cooling rack placed over a tray. Leave them to air-dry for at least 10 minutes, then dredge again.

Pour the cooking oil into a pan, preferably a medium wok, set over a medium heat. Fry the chicken at 160°C (320°F) in four or five batches. Fry for 5–6 minutes, then drain on a rack placed over a tray. After frying the last batch, fry the wings again, this time at 170°C (340°F) for 1½ minutes.

Pour the sriracha mixture into a large wok. Bring to the boil over a medium heat, then reduce the heat and simmer until the sauce leaves a thick track when you draw a spatula across the bottom of the pan.

Stir in the vinegar, then add all the wings and turn off the heat. Mix the wings until they are evenly coated with the sauce. Turn the heat to medium–low and cook for a couple of minutes, or until the sauce starts to dry out and brown in spots, stirring almost constantly.

Turn off the heat, then mix half the spring onions into the wings. Pile the wings on a plate and scatter the remaining spring onions on top.

MENTAIKO & SHISO-STUFFED WINGS

8 large mid-joint chicken wings with the
    wing tip
8 shiso leaves
8 small mentaiko sacs (see intro)
about 80g (2¾oz) coating mix
    (see page 162)
about 60ml (¼ cup) iced water
765ml (3⅓ cups) cooking oil
shichimi togarashi (Japanese seven spice)

Deboning chicken wings without cutting into the skin isn't difficult, but it does take some time. You'll get faster with practice, though – it used to take me a good 30 minutes to debone eight wings, and now I can do it in less than half that time. The trick is to use your paring knife sparingly, and cut only towards the bone, not towards the meat and skin. I use the knife only at the beginning, when I'm cutting the tendons around the top part of the bones, then again when I separate the two bones (the radius and ulna) at the top of the joint. Buy the largest mid-joint wings you can find, with the tip still attached. Larger wings are easier to debone than smaller ones, and they're easier to stuff.

Mentaiko is salted, spiced cod roe that is sold still in its thin, edible membrane. The sacs vary greatly in size: for this dish, buy small ones that weigh around 15g (½oz) each. If you can only find larger sacs, you'll need to scrape the tiny eggs out of the membrane, then shape the eggs into short, fat 'fingers' that you can stuff into the wings. Place the shaped mentaiko on a clingfilm/plastic wrap-lined tray and freeze until firm, but not frozen solid, before wrapping in the shiso leaf.

To make these wings, you also need sturdy wooden toothpicks and non-stick pan coating (cooking spray), which works better than oil at preventing things from sticking.

To debone the wings, place a paper towel on the cutting board – this prevents the wings from slipping. Use the tip of a paring knife to cut the tendons around the top of the mid-joint (the part where the drumette portion was). Make sure the knife tip is under the skin, and that you're cutting towards the bone. After cutting all of the tendons, stand the wing upright, with the wing tip on the cutting board and the mid-joint between your hands. Place the index finger of each hand on the outside of the two bones, and your thumbs between the bones. Holding the bones tightly, press firmly downwards with all digits at the same time so that the meat and skin tear away from the bones. Occasionally, you'll find a very tough tendon that needs to be cut – slice it carefully, again towards the bone. You should have a mid-joint that's stripped of the meat and skin, except for where it is still attached at the wing tip joint.

When the meat and skin are pushed down as far as possible, cut between the top part of the two bones, to separate them. Separately flex the two bones back and forth where they meet the wing tip, until you feel them snap away at the joint. Twist the thinner bone and push it out of the cavity – do not use the knife.

CONTINUED . . .

MENTAIKO & SHISO-STUFFED WINGS CONTINUED . . .

~~~~~~

Then, do the same with the larger bone. When finished, you'll have a wing tip attached to a boneless mid-joint. Lay the wings on a tray and refrigerate while preparing the filling.

Place the shiso leaves on a clean cutting board, with the stem end facing you. Cut a long, narrow notch in each leaf to remove the tough lower part of the midrib. Place a mentaiko sac on the leaf – perpendicular to the midrib – and roll it towards the tip of the leaf so it is fully enclosed. Repeat with the remaining shiso leaves and mentaiko sacs.

Spray 8 wooden toothpicks with non-stick pan coating (cooking spray). Spray a small rack placed over a tray.

Stuff the shiso/mentaiko rolls into the cavity of each wing and secure the opening with a toothpick. Lay the wings on the rack and refrigerate, uncovered, for at least 1 hour.

Put the coating mix in a bowl and add the iced water and 15ml (1 tablespoon) of the oil. Use a whisk to mix the ingredients. If necessary, drizzle in more iced water to create a batter that will coat the wings lightly and evenly.

Pour the remaining 750ml (3¼ cups) of cooking oil into a pan, preferably a medium wok, set over a medium heat. Working with four wings at a time, dip them one by one in the batter to coat them entirely. Hold the wings by the tip of the wing tip and lower into the hot oil. Fry the wings at 160°C (320°F) for 4–5 minutes, then remove from the oil and fry the remaining wings.

Fry the wings again at 170°C (340°F) for 1 minute. As soon as they've been fried a second time, sprinkle them liberally with shichimi togarashi (it's hard to make it stick – most of it will bounce off). Remove the toothpicks by twisting them to make sure they're not sticking, then pull them out of the wings.

To serve, slice each wing on the diagonal into three pieces, to show the pink and green filling. Spinkle with shichimi togarashi, to taste.

VIETNAMESE STUFFED WINGS

~~~~~~~~~~~~~~~~~~~~~~~~~~~~~~~~~~~~~ **Serves: 4–6**

30g (1oz) mung bean (glass) vermicelli
10g (⅓oz) dried cloud ear mushrooms
12 large mid-joint chicken wings with the
wing tip
2–3 peeled garlic cloves
75g (2½oz) peeled onion
45g (1½oz) carrot
60g (2oz) shelled prawn (shrimp) meat
120g (4¼oz) minced (ground) pork
15ml (1 tbsp) fish sauce
5g (1 tsp) coarse salt flakes
¾ tsp granulated sugar
1 tsp medium-grind black pepper
1 egg
750ml (3¼ cups) cooking oil

For brushing
45ml (3 tbsp) fish sauce
45g (3 tbsp) granulated sugar

For the dipping sauce
2–3 peeled garlic cloves
2–4 red bird's-eye chillies
30g (1oz) carrot
80ml (⅓ cup) fish sauce
25g (5 tsp) granulated sugar
30ml (2 tbsp) fresh lime juice
20ml (4 tsp) rice vinegar
30ml (2 tbsp) iced water

When I lived in San Francisco, I was fortunate to have Vietnamese friends who took me to the best Vietnamese restaurants in the city. They cooked for me, dared me to eat my first fertilized duck egg and were surprised that I liked it, and told me which takeaway shops had the best Banh Mi Thit. One of the restaurants they took me to served a delicious crab-stuffed chicken wing, which used the same filling as for their spring rolls. I stuff my wings (and spring rolls) with pork and prawns (shrimp), because there is only one person other than myself that I am willing to de-shell a crab for, and even then, I only do it to stop him from complaining.

Start making these wings (pictured on page 67) the day before you want to cook them, because they need to air-dry in the fridge for at least 8 hours. When the skin is dry and taut, it fries up crisper. The brushing sauce – a simple mixture of fish sauce and sugar – will ensure the skin turns an appetizing brown. The leftover filling can be used to make Vietnamese spring rolls: just roll the filling in rice paper that's been dipped briefly in cold water to rehydrate it. Double-fry the spring rolls until pale golden, and serve with lettuce leaves, fresh herbs, and the same dipping sauce used for the stuffed wings.

As in the previous recipe, you also need sturdy wooden toothpicks and non-stick pan coating (cooking spray), which works better than oil at preventing things from sticking.

Put the mung bean vermicelli and cloud ear mushrooms in a bowl and add plenty of water to cover them. Leave for about 30 minutes until hydrated.

While the ingredients are hydrating, debone the wings as directed on page 61. Put them in the fridge until the filling is ready.

Mince the garlic and onion, and coarsely grate the carrot. Drain the mung bean vermicelli and cloud ear mushrooms and squeeze out any excess water. Use scissors to cut the mung bean vermicelli into short lengths (no longer than 2.5cm/1in). Feel the cloud ear – sometimes there's a hard bit near the centre – remove it and discard. Mince the cloud ear and the prawns.

CONTINUED . . .

VIETNAMESE STUFFED WINGS CONTINUED . . .

Put the pork in a bowl and add the fish sauce, salt, sugar and black pepper. Mix well, then add the mung bean vermicelli, cloud ear mushrooms, garlic, onion, carrot and prawns. Combine thoroughly, then mix in the egg.

For the brushing liquid, stir together the fish sauce and granulated sugar, until the sugar is dissolved.

Spray 12 wooden toothpicks with non-stick pan coating (cooking spray). Spray a cooling rack placed over a tray.

Stuff some of the filling into each wing, pushing it down so it's evenly distributed. You'll need about 20g (¾oz) per wing, depending on the size. Secure the opening of each wing with a toothpick. Lay the wings on the rack. Brush the fish sauce/sugar mixture over each wing to coat it entirely. Place the wings, uncovered, in the fridge to air-dry for at least 8 hours, turning them over halfway, if necessary.

Before frying the wings, make the sauce. Mince the garlic. Cut the chillies into thin rounds, squeezing out and discarding the seeds as you go. Coarsely grate the carrot. Mix the fish sauce with the sugar until dissolved. Add the lime juice, vinegar, garlic, chillies and carrot, then dilute with the iced water. Taste the mixture and adjust the seasonings, if needed. If it's too strong, add more water. Set aside.

Pour the cooking oil into a pan, preferably a medium wok, set over a medium heat. Hold the wings by the tip of the wing tip and lower into the hot oil. Fry four wings at a time at 160°C (320°F) for 6–7 minutes, then lay them on the cooling rack placed over a tray. Fry the remaining wings the same way. After all the wings have been fried once, heat the oil again and fry them a second time at 170°C (340°F) for 1 minute.

Remove the toothpicks by twisting them to make sure they're not sticking, then pull them out. Arrange the wings on a platter and serve with the dipping sauce.

CHICKEN WINGS RELLENO

~~~~~~ **Serves: 4–6**

12 large mid-joint chicken wings with the
    wing tip
1 egg
60g (2oz) Filipino or Spanish chorizo
10g (⅓oz) gherkins (or pickles or
    cornichons)
10g (⅓oz) pitted green olives
10g (⅓oz) raisins
125g (4½oz) minced (ground) pork
5g (1 tsp) coarse salt flakes
½ tsp medium-grind black pepper
30g (1oz) potato or sweet potato flour
750ml (3¼ cups) cooking oil

Note
*You only need half a boiled egg for this
amount of filling.*

**Chicken Relleno, also called Chicken Rellenong, is a Filipino centre-
piece dish of a whole chicken that's been deboned then stuffed with
a savoury minced (ground) pork mixture studded with raisins, olives,
pickles and boiled egg, along with cured meats such as chorizo,
frankfurters and/or ham. The original version – of which there are
many variations – is baked, but for this dish, I use the meat mixture
and stuff it into deboned chicken wings, which are air-dried, then fried
(pictured on page 66). If possible, use a Filipino chorizo, but Spanish
chorizo is fine, too. Don't use Mexican chorizo, which is too soft.**

**As with the Mentaiko Wings (see page 61), you also need sturdy
wooden toothpicks and non-stick pan coating (cooking spray), which
works better than oil at preventing things from sticking.**

Debone the wings as directed on page 61. Put them in the fridge until the filling
is ready.

Put the egg in a small pan and add enough water to cover by 1cm (½in). Place
over a medium heat and bring to the boil, then cover the pan with the lid, turn
off the heat and leave for 12 minutes. Transfer the egg to a bowl filled with iced
water and leave until cold. Crack the egg and remove the shell.

Spray 12 wooden toothpicks with non-stick pan coating (cooking spray). Spray
a cooling rack placed over a tray.

Cut the chorizo, gherkins, olives and half of the hard-boiled egg into small dice
and place in a large bowl. Cut the raisins in half and add to the bowl, then add
the minced pork, the salt and pepper and mix thoroughly. Divide the mixture
into 12 even portions. Stuff one portion of the mixture into each wing and
secure the opening with a toothpick. Lay the wings on the rack and refrigerate
for at least 4 hours.

Dredge the wings in the potato or sweet potato flour, covering them
completely, then shake off the excess.

Pour the cooking oil into a pan, preferably a medium wok, set over a medium
heat. Fry the wings four at a time at 160°C (320°F) for 6–7 minutes. After frying
the last batch, re-fry the wings at 170°C (340°F) for 1½ minutes.

Remove the toothpicks by twisting them to make sure they're not sticking, then
pull them out. Arrange the wings on a platter and serve.

BONELESS LEGS

In the USA, I've eaten at specialist chicken restaurants that charge more if you ask for only the chicken breast, instead of their standard serving of a whole or half bird that, naturally enough, has both white and dark meat. I can't speak for all of Asia, but in Hong Kong, it's the opposite. People there tend to prefer dark meat, so if you order a plate of chicken rice and ask for the gai bei (chicken leg), they'll charge an extra HK$10 or more. It's a surcharge I gladly pay – I would much rather have the thigh and drumstick instead of the breast.

I like dark meat chicken because it has more flavour than the breast, and also because there's greater room for error when cooking it. When is the last time you ate a dry chicken thigh? I don't think that's ever happened to me – you'd have to be a pretty bad cook to overcook dark meat so much that it became dry. Boneless dark meat can tolerate a longer cooking time than breast meat, so the coating becomes darker and crunchier as it fries in the hot oil. A harder, crunchier coating doesn't become soggy as quickly when it's sauced, which is why I use dark meat for dishes such as Sweet and Sour Chicken (page 70) and Chicken Doubanjiang (page 97).

STRAWBERRY & PINEAPPLE SWEET & SOUR CHICKEN

Serves: 4–6

200g (7oz) peeled onion
200g (7oz) green banana chillies
30g (1oz) peeled garlic cloves
20g (¾oz) thinly sliced peeled ginger
700g (1lb 9oz) fresh pineapple, peeled and
   core removed (see note)
240g (8½oz) strawberry jam
120g (4¼oz) tomato purée (paste)
120ml (½ cup) unsweetened pineapple
   juice
180ml (¾ cup) rice vinegar
6–8 fresh strawberries, halved, to garnish

For coating and frying the chicken
800g (1lb 12oz) boneless chicken thighs
coarse salt flakes, as necessary
30ml (2 tbsp) soy sauce
   (all-purpose Kikkoman or your
   favourite brand)
20ml (4 tsp) rice wine
5g (1 tsp) granulated sugar
1 tsp finely ground white pepper
100g (3½oz) coating mix made with
   tapioca flour (see page 162)
about 40ml (2 tbsp + 2 tsp) iced water
20ml (4 tsp) coconut vinegar or distilled
   white vinegar
810ml (3½ cups) cooking oil
120g (4¼oz) tapioca flour

Note
*If the fresh pineapple is too acidic, sprinkle
it with salt (the exact amount doesn't matter)
after cutting it into chunks. Mix well, then
leave it in a colander for about 10 minutes.
Rinse it thoroughly before draining again.
The salt draws out the acidity and makes
it taste sweeter.*

Strawberry sweet and sour may sound like something dreamt up by a chef who's trying too hard to be creative, but it's not anything new: I first ate it in Hong Kong at least 25 years ago. I love this version of sweet and sour because the sauce is so much more complex than the type made with tomato ketchup, pineapple juice and white vinegar. Depending on the sweetness of the strawberry jam, you may need to add more vinegar to balance the flavours.

Butterfly the chicken thighs (see page 20), cut them into 3cm (1¼in) chunks and put them in a bowl. Weigh the chicken, then multiply the amount by 0.01 – this is the amount of salt you need. Sprinkle the salt over the chicken and mix well.

Add the soy sauce, rice wine, sugar and white pepper. Combine thoroughly, then set aside to marinate at room temperature for at least 30 minutes.

Halve the onion, then thinly slice it. Slice the banana chillies on the diagonal. Halve the garlic cloves and slice them, then julienne the ginger. Cut the pineapple into bite-sized chunks. In a food processor, blend the strawberry jam and tomato purée until smooth. Transfer to a bowl and stir in the pineapple juice and vinegar. Taste the sauce and add more vinegar, if necessary. Set aside.

Put the coating mix into a bowl and add the iced water, vinegar and 20ml (4 teaspoons) of the oil. Whisk until smooth, then pour this over the chicken and mix well to create a batter that coats the pieces lightly and evenly. If necessary, adjust the consistency by adding a little more water.

Dredge the battered chicken pieces in the tapioca flour and lay them on a cooling rack placed over a tray. Leave to air-dry for at least 10 minutes, then dredge the pieces again.

Pour 750ml (3¼ cups) of the cooking oil into a pan, preferably a medium wok, set over a medium heat. Fry the chicken at 160°C (320°F) in four or five batches. Fry for 3–4 minutes, then drain on the rack placed over the tray. After frying the last batch, fry the chicken again, this time at 170°C (340°F) for 1½ minutes.

Heat 30ml (2 tablespoons) of fresh oil in a large wok set over a medium–high heat. Add the onion and banana chilli and stir-fry for about 30 seconds, or until the onion starts to soften. Remove the ingredients from the wok.

Pour the remaining 10ml (2 teaspoons) oil into the wok and place over a high heat. Add the garlic and ginger and stir-fry briefly, then add the jam mixture and the pineapple. Bring to the boil and cook until the liquid is reduced by three quarters.

Reduce the heat to medium. Add the chicken, onion and banana chillies, then stir to lightly coat the chicken with the sauce. To serve, garnish with the strawberries.

TAMARIND CHICKEN

〜〜〜〜〜〜〜〜〜〜〜〜〜〜〜〜〜〜〜〜〜〜〜〜 **Serves: 4–6**

200g (7oz) peeled shallots
8–12 red bird's-eye chillies
8–12 spring onions (scallions)
80g (⅓ cup) tamarind paste
30ml (2 tbsp) fish sauce
30g (2 tbsp) granulated sugar
750ml (3¼ cups) cooking oil
150g (5½oz) unsalted cashews

For seasoning and coating the chicken
800g (1lb 12oz) boneless chicken thighs
coarse salt flakes, as necessary
30ml (2 tbsp) soy sauce
    (all-purpose Kikkoman or your
    favourite brand)
2 tsp finely ground white pepper
120g (4¼oz) coating mix (see page 162)

This dish is irresistible, with the sweet-tart flavour of the tamarind-glazed chicken enhanced by plenty of fried shallots and the crunchy texture of the fried cashews. When frying shallots, watch them carefully, especially as soon as they take on a hint of colour, because they go from just right to burnt in the blink of an eye.

Butterfly the chicken thighs (see page 20), cut them into strips about 1.25cm (½in) wide and put the pieces in a bowl. Weigh the chicken, then multiply the amount by 0.01 – this is the amount of salt you need. Sprinkle the salt over the chicken and mix well, then add the soy sauce and white pepper.

Halve the shallots, then thinly slice them. Cut the bird's-eye chillies into thin rings, shaking out and discarding the seeds as you go. Mince the spring onions and divide them into two portions. Mix the tamarind paste with the fish sauce and sugar. Set aside.

Pour the cooking oil into a pan, preferably a medium wok, set over a medium heat. Add the shallots and fry at around 130°C (265°F). Stir often and watch them carefully. As soon as they start to take on the slightest colour, corral them into a wide, shallow mesh strainer or sieve so they are ready to lift out of the oil as soon as they darken. Continue to fry them, stirring them while they are still in the strainer, until they are pale golden. Watch them very carefully and as soon as they darken just a little more, lift them out of the oil. Place the strainer over a bowl and let the shallots drain.

Heat the oil again, then add the cashews and fry at 150°C (300°F) for about 1 minute, or until toasted. Take them out of the oil, then drain on paper towels.

Add the coating mix to the chicken and mix well – the meat should look dry, with no damp patches. Shake off the excess coating mix.

Heat the oil again and fry the chicken at 160°C (320°F) in four or five batches. After adding the chicken to the oil, use long chopsticks to separate the pieces. Fry for 4 minutes, then drain on a cooling rack placed over a tray. After frying all the chicken, fry the pieces a second time at 170°C (340°F) for 1 minute.

Very lightly coat a large wok with fresh oil, then place it over a medium–low heat. Pour in the tamarind mixture and simmer until syrupy, stirring often. Mix in the chillies, then stir in the fried shallots and half the spring onions. Turn off the heat and add the chicken. Stir the ingredients so the chicken is lightly coated with the tamarind glaze and other ingredients. If the chicken pieces seem too damp, turn on the heat to low and stir constantly until the glaze dries out slightly.

Mix in the cashews, then transfer to a serving plate. Scatter with the remaining spring onions before serving.

BONELESS LEGS

CHICKEN WITH SPRING ONION & GINGER SAUCE

Serves: 4–6

800g (1lb 12oz) boneless chicken thighs
coarse salt flakes, as necessary
5g (1 tsp) granulated sugar
1 tsp finely ground white pepper
1 tsp five-spice powder
20ml (4 tsp) rice wine
100g (3½oz) coating mix (see page 162)
about 60ml (¼ cup) iced water
120g (4¼oz) tapioca flour
750ml (3¼ cups) cooking oil

For the spring onion and ginger sauce
240g (8½oz) spring onions (scallions)
about 120g (4¼oz) chunk of peeled ginger
   (use as necessary)
10g (2 tsp) coarse salt flakes
90g (3oz) rendered chicken fat
   (or cooking oil)

Chinese spring onion (scallion) and ginger sauce is a delicious condiment that makes any simply cooked meat taste better, but it goes especially well with chicken. It couldn't be easier to make – it's just minced spring onions, grated ginger and salt, along with some fat that you heat and drizzle over the ingredients to make them sizzle. I like it best when made with Rendered Chicken Fat (see page 163), but if you don't have any, it's still good if you use plain cooking oil. Add the grated ginger to taste.

Butterfly the chicken thighs (see page 20), cut them into 2.5cm (1in) chunks and put them in a bowl. Weigh the chicken, then multiply the amount by 0.01 – this is the amount of salt you need. Sprinkle the salt over the chicken and mix well. Mix in the sugar, pepper, five-spice powder and rice wine and leave to marinate at room temperature for at least 30 minutes.

For the spring onion and ginger sauce, finely mince the spring onions and put them in a bowl. Use a fine grater – preferably a ceramic oroshigane, see page 17 – to grate the chunk of ginger into a fine purée. Use 45g–60g (1½–2oz) of the ginger purée, or to taste. Mix the salt into the spring onions and ginger. Heat the chicken fat (or oil) to 160°C (320°F) and pour it over the ingredients – it will sizzle. Mix well, then set aside to cool.

Sprinkle the coating mix over the chicken, add the iced water and mix to create a batter that lightly coats the meat. If necessary, adjust the consistency by adding more iced water.

Dredge the battered chicken pieces in the tapioca flour and lay them on a cooling rack placed over a tray. Leave to air-dry for at least 10 minutes, then dredge the pieces again.

Pour the cooking oil into a pan, preferably a medium wok, set over a medium heat. Fry the chicken at 160°C (320°F) in four or five batches. Fry for 2 minutes, then drain on the rack placed over the tray. After frying the last batch, fry the chicken again, this time at 170°C (340°F) for 1½ minutes.

Put the chicken pieces in a bowl, add about two-thirds of the spring onion and ginger sauce, to taste, and mix well. Pile the pieces onto a dish and serve the rest of the spring onion and ginger sauce on the side.

KOREAN FIRE CHICKEN

Serves: 4–6

800g (1lb 12oz) boneless chicken thighs

15g (½oz) peeled garlic cloves

10g (⅓oz) thinly sliced peeled ginger

45g (1½oz) gochujang (Korean chilli paste)

15g (1 tbsp) granulated sugar

20g (¾oz) golden syrup (or corn syrup)

20g (¾oz) gochugaru (Korean chilli flakes),
  or more to taste

30ml (2 tbsp) soy sauce
  (all-purpose Kikkoman or your
  favourite brand)

5ml (1 tsp) sesame oil

½ tsp coarse salt flakes

about 120g (4¼oz) coating mix
  (see page 162)

750ml (3¼ cups) cooking oil

2–3 spring onions (scallions)

Despite its name, fire chicken isn't nearly as spicy as you might think, unless you have a particularly sensitive palate. In fact, I'm sure there are some people out there who will think this is too mild – they can increase the amount of gochugaru, if they like. This chicken is great with beer or soju (Korean distilled alcoholic beverage), because its strong flavour goes well with alcohol. I like to serve this chicken with pickled radish (see page 166).

Butterfly the chicken thighs (see page 20), cut them into 2.5cm (1in) chunks and put them in a bowl. Finely mince the garlic and ginger and mix them into the chicken. Add the gochujang, sugar, syrup, gochugaru, soy sauce, sesame oil and salt and mix well. Marinate the chicken at room temperature for about 2 hours, stirring occasionally.

Dredge the chicken pieces in the coating mix and shake off any excess. Lay the pieces on a cooling rack placed over a tray. Leave them to air-dry for at least 10 minutes, then dredge again.

Pour the cooking oil into a pan, preferably a medium wok, set over a medium heat. Fry the chicken at 160°C (320°F) in four or five batches. Fry for 2 minutes, then drain on the rack placed over the tray. After frying the last batch, fry the chicken again, this time at 170°C (340°F) for 1½ minutes.

Mince the spring onions, then scatter them over the chicken on a large plate to serve.

THAI CRUNCHY CHICKEN WITH TOASTED RICE POWDER

Serves: 4–6

800g (1lb 12oz) boneless chicken thighs
30ml (2 tbsp) fish sauce
30ml (2 tbsp) soy sauce
(all-purpose Kikkoman or your
favourite brand)
20g (4 tsp) granulated sugar
90g (3oz) toasted rice powder (see intro)
2 tsp Thai chilli flakes
18 pairs of makrut lime leaves
about 100g (3½oz) coating mix
(see page 162)
750ml (3¼ cups) cooking oil

This is another delicious Thai recipe from my friend Tass. She usually makes it with pork neck, but when I cooked it for her using chicken, she nodded in approval.

Toasted rice powder is used in Thai dishes to add flavour and texture. You can buy it in shops specializing in Thai ingredients, but it's easy to make. Put about 150g (5½oz) of uncooked glutinous rice grains in a dry (unoiled) frying pan (skillet) placed over a low–medium heat. Shake the pan back and forth almost constantly, and occasionally mix the rice with a spoon or spatula. Cook until the rice grains are pale to medium-brown. Cool the rice, then use a blender or pestle and mortar to grind it to a slightly coarse powder. Store in an airtight container.

Butterfly the chicken thighs (see page 20), then cut them into strips about 1.25cm (½in) wide. Put the chicken in a bowl and mix in the fish sauce, soy sauce, sugar, toasted rice powder and chilli flakes. Separate 12 pairs of the lime leaves into individual leaves, then tear out or cut out the midribs. Stack the leaves, then cut them as thinly as possible. Blot the remaining lime leaves with a paper towel to remove excess moisture and separate the pairs into individual leaves. Add the julienned lime leaves to the chicken, stir well, then marinate at room temperature for at least 1 hour.

Sprinkle the coating mix over the chicken and mix well. The chicken should look dry, with no damp spots. Shake off the excess coating mix.

Pour the cooking oil into a pan, preferably a medium wok, set over a medium heat. Fry the chicken at 160°C (320°F) in four or five batches. Fry the pieces for 4–5 minutes, then drain them on a cooling rack placed over a tray – there's no need to fry them a second time.

Add the individual lime leaves to the hot oil and fry them until they curl slightly, then use them to garnish the chicken.

MARGARITA FORÉS' FRIED CHICKEN INASAL

Serves: 4–6

800g (1lb 12oz) boneless chicken thighs
4–6 peeled garlic cloves
20g (¾oz) peeled red onion
10g (⅓oz) galangal
10g (⅓oz) lemongrass (lower 8cm/3¼in
   of the stalks)
120ml (½ cup) coconut vinegar
15ml (1 tbsp) soy sauce
   (all-purpose Kikkoman or your
   favourite brand)
5g (1 tsp) coarse salt flakes
25g (5 tsp) soft brown sugar
120g (4¼oz) coating mix made with
   tapioca flour (see page 162)
20ml (4 tsp) annatto oil (see below)
120g (4¼oz) tapioca flour
750ml (3¼ cups) cooking oil
calamansi limes (or Thai limes), to serve

For the annatto oil

125g (4½oz) chicken fat and skin
1 peeled garlic clove
1 tbsp annatto seeds

Note

*Making this annatto oil is very much like
making Rendered Chicken Fat (see page 163).
Whenever I cook a whole chicken, I pull out
the excess fat from the cavity, and remove the
skin from the neck. I freeze the fat and skin and
when I have enough, I make rendered chicken
fat or this annatto oil. If you have a friendly
neighbourhood butcher, you could also ask
them to give you (or sell cheaply) any spare
chicken fat and skin they might have.*

I first met Margarita Forés at an event for Asia's 50 Best Restaurants,
when she won the award for Asia's Best Female Chef 2016. We quickly
bonded over our love for food.

When I was writing this book, I asked her if she had any good Filipino
chicken recipes, and she very generously gave me her family's
recipe for chicken Inasal. Traditionally, it is a dish of grilled chicken,
which doesn't work for the theme of this book, so I experimented
with making a fried version. Something magical happened with the
combination of vinegar (in the marinade), annatto oil and my usual
coating mix, to make the crunchiest chicken ever.

Butterfly the chicken thighs (see page 20), cut them into 2.5cm (1in) chunks and
put them in a bowl. Thinly slice the garlic, onion and galangal. Use the flat side
of a metal meat mallet to bash the lower 8cm (3¼in) of the lemongrass stalk,
then slice it as thinly as possible. Put the garlic, onion, galangal, and 10g (⅓oz)
lemongrass in the bowl with the chicken and add the vinegar, soy sauce, salt
and sugar. Mix well, then leave to marinate in the fridge for 8–12 hours, stirring
occasionally.

To make the annatto oil, cut the chicken fat and skin into small pieces and put
them in a pan. Slice the garlic clove and put it in the pan along with the annatto
seeds and about 15ml (1 tablespoon) of water. Place over a medium heat and
cook until it starts to sizzle, then reduce the heat and cook until the fat renders
out, stirring occasionally. Strain the mixture through a sieve placed over a bowl.
(Don't throw away the chicken cracklings – they are delicious!)

Add the coating mix to the bowl with the chicken and marinade and mix well.
Add 20ml (4 teaspoons) of the annatto oil and mix again to create a batter that
coats the chicken lightly and evenly. If necessary, adjust the consistency of the
batter by mixing in more coating mix or some iced water.

Dredge the battered chicken in the tapioca flour, then lay the pieces on
a cooling rack placed over a tray. Leave them to air-dry for at least 10 minutes.

Pour the cooking oil into a pan, preferably a medium wok, set over a medium
heat. Fry the chicken at 160°C (320°F) in four or five batches. Fry the pieces for
2 minutes, then drain on a rack placed over a tray. After frying the last batch, fry
the chicken again, this time at 170°C (340°F) for 1½ minutes.

Drizzle some annatto oil over the chicken before serving with halved calamansi
limes (or Thai limes, cut as directed on page 15).

CHICKEN KARAAGE

Serves: 4–6

800g (1lb 12oz) boneless chicken thighs
3–5 peeled garlic cloves
15g (½oz) chunk of peeled ginger
40ml (2 tbsp + 2 tsp) soy sauce
    (all-purpose Kikkoman or your
    favourite brand)
30ml (2 tbsp) mirin
20ml (4 tsp) sake
5g (1 tsp) granulated sugar
5g (1 tsp) coarse salt flakes
1 tsp finely ground white pepper
10ml (2 tsp) sesame oil
about 100g (3½oz) coating mix made with
    potato flour (see page 162)
about 120g (4¼oz) potato flour
750ml (3¼ cups) cooking oil

Chicken Karaage is one of the most popular of all Japanese dishes. Japanese parents make it at home to tuck into their children's bento boxes, it's sold at convenience stores throughout Japan, and you don't even have to look at the menu of an izakaya anywhere in the world to know that you can order a plate of piping hot chicken Karaage. It's not difficult to make, and I like it so much that I occasionally fry up a whole batch just for myself so I can have leftovers for a couple of days. I like to eat it with shredded cabbage and Japanese Potato Salad (see page 170).

Butterfly the chicken thighs (see page 20), cut them into 2.5cm (1in) chunks and put them in a bowl.

Use a fine grater – preferably a ceramic oroshigane, see page 17 – to grate the garlic and ginger to a smooth purée. Put the garlic and ginger into a bowl and mix in the soy sauce, mirin, sake, sugar, salt, pepper and sesame oil. Add this to the chicken and mix well, then leave to marinate at room temperature for about 2 hours.

Sprinkle the coating mix over the chicken and mix to create a batter that lightly coats the meat. If necessary, adjust the consistency by adding some iced water. Dredge the battered chicken in the potato flour and shake off the excess, then put the pieces on a cooling rack placed over a tray. Leave them to air-dry for at least 10 minutes.

Pour the cooking oil into a pan, preferably a medium wok, set over a medium heat. Fry the chicken at 160°C (320°F) in four or five batches. Fry for 2 minutes, then drain on the rack placed over the tray. After frying the last batch, fry the chicken again, this time at 170°C (340°F) for 1½ minutes.

Pile the pieces on a plate and serve.

CHICKEN CUTLETS WITH CANTONESE CURRY SAUCE

Serves: 4–6

8 boneless chicken thighs,
  about 120g (4¼oz) each
coarse salt flakes, as necessary
1 tsp finely ground white pepper
40ml (2 tbsp + 2 tsp) rice wine
about 120g (4¼oz) potato or sweet
  potato flour
3–4 eggs
about 160g (5¾oz) panko breadcrumbs
600ml (generous 2½ cups) cooking oil
cooked rice, as needed

For the curry sauce
800g (1lb 12oz) all-purpose potatoes
200g (7oz) peeled onion
30g (1oz) peeled garlic cloves
20g (¾oz) thinly sliced peeled ginger
60ml (¼ cup) cooking oil
10g (⅓oz) curry powder (see note)
½–1 tsp Tianjin chilli powder, or to taste
40g (1½oz) plain (all-purpose) flour
200ml (scant 1 cup) evaporated milk
20g (4 tsp) granulated sugar
60ml (¼ cup) fish sauce
20ml (4 tsp) soy sauce
  (all-purpose Kikkoman or your
  favourite brand)
60g (2oz) golden syrup (or corn syrup)

Note
*Choose your curry powder carefully because
it can vary a lot in taste and spice level,
depending on the producer. If possible, look
for a brand that's made in Hong Kong, such
as Koon Yick Wah Kee.*

There's a restaurant in Hong Kong that I just love – Sun King Yuen.
It has an extensive menu but I've never even glanced at it because
I order only one thing: the Curry Pork Chop Rice. It's a huge portion of
wonderfully tender, lightly breaded fried pork chop served over rice,
with a side bowl of curry sauce with a single potato in it. I decided to
make a version of it, but using chicken in place of the pork, and panko
instead of Sun King Yuen's softer coating. I also wanted to add more
potatoes to the sauce because one is just not enough. This makes
more curry sauce than you'll need for the chicken. Store the leftovers
in the fridge and use within about 10 days.

Butterfly the chicken thighs (see page 20) and put them in a bowl. Weigh the
chicken, then multiply the amount by 0.015 – this is the amount of salt you need.
Sprinkle the salt and pepper over the chicken, then drizzle with the rice wine and
rub it into the meat. Set aside at room temperature while you prepare the sauce.

Peel the potatoes then cut them into 4cm (1½in) chunks. Put the potatoes in
a pan of salted water and place over a medium heat. Bring to the boil, then
reduce the heat, simmer for 3 minutes, then drain in a colander.

Mince the onion, garlic and ginger. Heat the cooking oil for the curry sauce in
a pan set over a low heat, then add the onion, garlic and ginger. Stir frequently
until the onion starts to soften, then add the curry and chilli powders. Stir for
30 seconds, then sprinkle in the plain flour. Stir constantly for 2 minutes – it will
be quite dry. Add 1 litre (4⅓ cups) of water a little at a time, using a whisk to stir
well. After adding all the water, whisk in the evaporated milk, sugar, fish sauce,
soy sauce and syrup. Bring to the boil, then reduce the heat and simmer for
5 minutes. Add the potatoes and simmer for 5–10 minutes, or until they are
soft, and the sauce is a good consistency. Taste for seasonings and adjust if
necessary, then turn off the heat.

Put the potato or sweet potato flour in a shallow dish. Whisk the eggs in another
shallow dish and put the panko in a third dish. Dredge the chicken thighs in the
flour, shake off the excess, then dip in the egg. Dredge in the panko, pressing
firmly so the breadcrumbs adhere.

Pour the cooking oil for the chicken into a 28cm (11¼in) frying pan (skillet),
preferably cast iron, set over a medium heat. Fry the chicken at 160°C (320°F)
for 6–8 minutes, turning over the pieces as necessary. Drain the chicken on
a cooling rack placed over a tray.

Reheat the sauce and thin it by whisking in some water, if necessary. Cut the
chicken into strips about 1cm (½in) wide; serve with the cooked rice, and curry
sauce on the side.

FRIED CHICKEN WITH FERMENTED BEANCURD

Serves: 4–6

800g (1lb 12oz) boneless chicken thighs

4–6 peeled garlic cloves

4–6 red bird's-eye chillies

80g (2¾oz) fermented beancurd (fu yu)

10g (2 tsp) granulated sugar

5g (1 tsp) coarse salt flakes

20ml (4 tsp) soy sauce
   (all-purpose Kikkoman or your
   favourite brand)

20ml (4 tsp) rice wine

about 100g (3½oz) coating mix
   (see page 162)

about 100g (3½oz) water chestnut flour

750ml (3¼ cups) cooking oil

Fermented beancurd is sometimes called Chinese cheese, although it's made of soybeans, not milk. It's made by drying, salting and fermenting fresh beancurd, then soaking it in a seasoned brine. There are two basic types of fermented beancurd: fu yu and nam yu. They start off life the same way, but nam yu is fermented in a brine that contains red rice wine lees (the solid residue leftover from making rice wine), giving the beancurd a reddish tinge and stronger flavour. For this dish, you want fu yu, which is pale beige.

Butterfly the chicken thighs (see page 20), cut them into 3cm (1¼in) chunks and put them in a bowl. Finely mince the garlic. Slice the chillies into thin rings, shaking out and discarding the seeds as you go. Use a fork to mash the beancurd with the sugar and salt in a bowl. Stir in the soy sauce, rice wine, garlic and chillies, then pour the mixture over the chicken and mix thoroughly. Marinate at room temperature for about 2 hours, mixing occasionally.

Sprinkle the coating mix over the chicken in the bowl and mix well to make a batter that clings gently to the meat.

Put the water chestnut flour in a food processor or blender and process it until it is lump free, then transfer it to a shallow dish. Dredge the battered chicken in the water chestnut flour, pressing firmly so it adheres. Put the pieces on a cooling rack placed over a tray and leave them to air-dry for at least 10 minutes.

Pour the cooking oil into a pan, preferably a medium wok, set over a medium heat. Fry the chicken at 160°C (320°F) in four or five batches. Fry for 3–4 minutes, then drain on the rack placed over the tray. After frying the last batch, fry the chicken again, this time at 170°C (340°F) for 1½ minutes.

Pile the chicken into a bowl and serve hot or warm.

LEMONGRASS & MAKRUT LIME LEAF CHICKEN

Serves: 4–6

800g (1lb 12oz) boneless chicken thighs
coarse salt flakes, as necessary
16–20 pairs of makrut lime leaves
30g (1oz) lemongrass (the lower 8cm/3¼in
of the stalks)
60g (2oz) spring onions (scallions)
1 tbsp Thai chilli flakes
60g (¼ cup) oyster sauce
40ml (2 tbsp + 2 tsp) fish sauce
5g (1 tsp) granulated sugar
100g (3½oz) coating mix (see page 162)
about 60ml (¼ cup) iced water
120g (4¼oz) potato, sweet potato or
tapioca flour
750ml (3¼ cups) cooking oil

Both lemongrass and makrut lime leaf add a lovely, refreshing lift to whatever they are cooked with.

Butterfly the chicken thighs (see page 20), cut them into 2.5cm (1in) chunks and put them in a bowl. Weigh the chicken, then multiply the amount by 0.01 – this is the amount of salt you need. Sprinkle the salt over the chicken and mix well.

Separate the pairs of lime leaves, then tear out or cut out the midrib. Stack the leaves, then shred them as finely as possible. Use a metal meat mallet to bash the lower 8cm (3¼in) of 2–3 lemongrass stalks, then finely slice. Mince the spring onions. Add the lime leaves, 30g (1oz) lemongrass, spring onions, chilli flakes, oyster sauce, fish sauce and sugar to the chicken, mix thoroughly, then marinate at room temperature for about 2 hours.

Sprinkle the coating mix over the chicken, add the iced water and mix to create a batter that lightly coats the meat. If necessary, adjust the consistency by adding more iced water. Dredge the pieces in the potato, sweet potato or tapioca flour then lay them on a cooling rack placed over a tray.

Pour the cooking oil into a pan, preferably a medium wok, set over a medium heat. Fry the chicken at 160°C (320°F) in four or five batches. Fry for 3–4 minutes, then drain on the cooling rack placed over the tray. After frying the last batch, fry the chicken again, this time at 170°C (340°F) for 1½ minutes.

Pile the chicken pieces into a bowl and serve hot or warm.

PANDAN CHICKEN

600g (1lb 5oz) boneless chicken thighs
coarse salt flakes, as necessary
4 peeled garlic cloves
15g (½oz) coriander (cilantro) root with
  about 2.5cm (1in) of the stem
  (see page 14)
30g (2 tbsp) oyster sauce
15ml (1 tbsp) soy sauce
  (all-purpose Kikkoman or your
  favourite brand)
10ml (2 tsp) sesame oil
10g (2 tsp) granulated sugar
1 tsp finely ground white pepper
30ml (2 tbsp) canned coconut milk
24–30 pandan leaves, about 4cm (1½in)
  wide at the widest point
750ml (3¼ cups) cooking oil

For the sauce
50g (1¾oz) bottled Thai sweet chilli sauce
50g (1¾oz) sriracha
20ml (4 tsp) white vinegar

This popular restaurant dish looks difficult to prepare, primarily because of the way the chicken is wrapped in the pandan leaves in what seems to be a complex series of moves. Actually, it's much harder to describe than to do. If you can't understand my instructions, look up a video on YouTube.

Butterfly the chicken thighs (see page 20), cut them into 1.25cm (½in) pieces and put them in a bowl. Weigh the chicken, then multiply the amount by 0.01 – this is the amount of salt you need. Sprinkle the salt over the chicken and mix well.

Roughly chop the garlic and coriander root, then put them into a mortar and pound to a paste with the pestle. Put the paste in a bowl and mix in the oyster sauce, soy sauce, sesame oil, sugar, pepper and coconut milk. Add this mixture to the chicken, stir well, then marinate for 4–24 hours in the fridge.

Take the firm end of a pandan leaf in your left hand with the shiny side up and the pointy end facing the right (if you're right-handed) and run your fingers along it to make it more flexible; take care not to break it. Fold the leaf off centre, about 12cm (4½in) from the wide end, and shape it into a small, loose cone with the short side crossing in a 'V' in front of the long, pointy side. Tuck the tip of the pointy end into the hole at the bottom of the cone and pull it partially through, so it forms a loop on top, then bring it up the back so you're holding it behind the 'V'.

Holding the cone together securely with your left hand, put some of the chicken mixture in the leaf, filling the cone about three-quarters full. Carefully pull the pointy end through the hole at the bottom of the cone to secure the filling and adjust the short side of the leaf so the hole in the bottom is tightly closed. If necessary, tighten the loop to fully enclose the meat by pulling on alternate sides gently. Pull the pointy end up the back part of the parcel, then up and over. Insert the pointy end through a flap in the front of the parcel and pull tightly – the meat should be enclosed securely, with a little of it showing at the top. Trim off the pointy end of the leaf flush with the parcel, cutting it close to the parcel, and cut the shorter end into a point about 3cm (1¼in) from the end, so it can be used as a handle. Repeat with the remaining meat and leaves. You should end up with 24–30 roughly trapezium/trapezoid-shaped parcels.

Pour the cooking oil into a pan, preferably a medium wok, set over a medium heat. Fry the parcels in batches, cooking them at 160°C (320°F) for about 5 minutes. The oil will splatter a lot at the beginning. When the parcels are cooked, drain them upright on a cooling rack placed over a tray.

To make the sauce, mix the sweet chilli sauce with the sriracha and vinegar. Taste the mixture and adjust the seasonings, if necessary.

Serve the pandan chicken with the dipping sauce on the side.

BONELESS LEGS

CHICKEN POPPERS WITH INSTANT NOODLE COATING

Serves: 4–6
as a snack

450g (1lb) boneless chicken thighs
coarse salt crystals, as necessary
2–4 packets of instant noodles,
    depending on size
about 60g (2oz) potato, sweet potato
    or tapioca flour
2–3 eggs
750ml (3¼ cups) cooking oil

I came up with the idea for this dish after listening to two friends talk about instant noodles – a subject that is dear to my stomach. Peter reminisced about eating instant noodles, sprinkled with the seasoning mix, straight out of the packet, without cooking them first. Carol said that she hadn't ever tasted one of my favourite instant noodles, Nongshim Shin Ramyun. I wondered how instant noodles would work as a coating for fried chicken, and fortunately had a packet of Nongshim Shin Ramyun in my cupboard. (An important tip if you want to buy these: seek out the ones made in South Korea, because they taste so much better than the ones made elsewhere.) It was one of the easiest fried chicken dishes I've made, and the noodles fried up spicy and crunchy. You can vary the flavour by using other types of instant noodles, but make sure the seasoning packet is a dry mix, not a paste. Also, use only the seasoning powder, not any oil or dehydrated vegetables that may come in the packet.

This fried chicken goes very well with soju (Korean distilled alcoholic beverage) or beer.

Butterfly the chicken thighs (see page 20), cut them into 2.5cm (1in) chunks and put them in a bowl. Weigh the chicken, then multiply the amount by 0.005 – this is the amount of salt you need. Sprinkle the salt over the chicken, mix well, then set aside for at least 10 minutes.

Put the noodles with the contents of the dry seasoning pack in a food processor. Process until the noodles are about the size of rice grains.

Put the potato, sweet potato or tapioca flour in a shallow dish. Whisk the eggs in another shallow dish and put the instant noodles in a third dish. Dredge the chicken thighs in the flour and shake off the excess, then dip in the egg. Dredge in the instant noodles, pressing firmly so they adhere. Lay the chicken on a cooling rack placed over a tray.

Pour the cooking oil into a pan, preferably a medium wok, set over a medium heat. Fry the chicken in two batches at 160°C (320°F). Fry the pieces for 4 minutes, then put them on the rack placed over the tray – there's no need to fry again.

TORIKATSU

6 boneless chicken thighs, about
  120g (4¼oz) each
coarse salt flakes, as necessary
about 100g (3½oz) potato or sweet
  potato flour
2–3 eggs
about 120g (4¼oz) panko breadcrumbs
600ml (generous 2½ cups) cooking oil

For the Torikatsu sauce
180g (6¼oz) tomato ketchup
120–180ml (½–¾ cup) Worcestershire
  sauce
40ml (2 tbsp + 2 tsp) soy sauce
  (all-purpose Kikkoman or your
  favourite brand)
40–50g (1½–1¾oz) honey
5ml (1 tsp) sesame oil

Torikatsu is the chicken version of Tonkatsu, or breaded, fried pork. It's made in a similar way, with a crisp, panko coating, is served with the same Worcestershire-based sauce, and with the same accompaniments of short-grain rice, shredded cabbage, Japanese (or Colman's) mustard and miso soup.

Butterfly the chicken thighs (see page 20) and put them in a bowl. Weigh the chicken, then multiply the amount by 0.015 – this is the amount of salt you need. Sprinkle the salt over the chicken and mix well.

To make the Torikatsu sauce, put all the ingredients in a pan and bring to the boil over a medium heat. Simmer for about 1 minute, then taste for seasonings and add more Worcestershire sauce, if you like. Set aside to cool to room temperature.

Put the flour in a shallow dish. Whisk the eggs in another shallow dish and put the panko in a third dish. Dredge the chicken thighs in the flour and shake off the excess, then dip in the egg. Dredge in the panko, pressing firmly so the breadcrumbs adhere. Lay the chicken on a cooling rack placed over a tray.

Pour the cooking oil into a 28cm (11¼in) frying pan (skillet), preferably cast iron, set over a medium heat. Fry the chicken at 160°C (320°F) for 6–8 minutes, turning the pieces over once. Drain the chicken on the rack placed over the tray. There's no need to re-fry the chicken.

Cut the chicken into strips about 1cm (½in) wide, then either serve with the Torikatsu sauce on the side or drizzled over.

GARLICKY NUGGETS WITH SPRING ONION BATTER

Serves: 4–6

800g (1lb 12oz) boneless chicken thighs
coarse salt flakes, as necessary
20g (¾oz) peeled garlic cloves
30ml (2 tbsp) rice wine
10g (2 tsp) granulated sugar
1 tsp finely ground white pepper
1½ tsp garlic powder
750ml (3¼ cups) cooking oil

For the batter
120g (4¼oz) spring onions (scallions)
100g (3½oz) coating mix (see page 162)
1 tsp garlic powder
10g (⅓oz) gochugaru (Korean chilli flakes)
about 40ml (2 tbsp + 2 tsp) iced water
20ml (4 tsp) cooking oil
20ml (4 tsp) coconut vinegar or distilled
    white vinegar

I made these chicken nuggets when I had some friends over for a casual dinner. I set the bowl of nuggets on the table for them to eat while I prepared the main dishes, then went into the kitchen for just a few minutes. When I went back to the dining room, the nuggets were gone. I thought they were paying a trick on me and hiding the nuggets, but it turns out they just really liked them. The nuggets go well with Mac Salad and Sesame Garlic Cucumbers (see pages 171 and 167).

Butterfly the chicken thighs (see page 20), cut them into 3cm (1¼in) chunks and put them in a bowl. Weigh the chicken, then multiply the amount by 0.015 – this is the amount of salt you need. Sprinkle the salt over the chicken and mix well.

Use a fine grater – preferably a ceramic oroshigane, see page 17 – to grate the garlic to a smooth purée, then put it in the bowl with the chicken. Mix in the rice wine, sugar, pepper and garlic powder. Leave to marinate for at least 1 hour at room temperature.

To make the batter, mince the spring onions. Put the coating mix into a bowl and whisk in the garlic powder and gochugaru. Add the iced water, oil and vinegar and whisk to combine. Stir in the spring onions. Pour the batter over the chicken and mix well. The batter should be a little thicker than usual – it should thoroughly coat the chicken and spring onions. If necessary, mix in more iced water.

Pour the cooking oil into a pan, preferably a medium wok, set over a medium heat. Use two spoons to scoop up the coated chicken pieces, making sure you get spring onions in every spoonful, and gently slide the mixture into the hot oil. Fry the chicken at 160ºC (320ºF) in four or five batches. Fry the pieces for 4 minutes, then drain them on a cooling rack placed over a tray. After frying the last batch, fry the chicken again, this time at 170ºC (340ºF) for about 1½ minutes.

Pile into a bowl and serve.

CHICKEN DOUBANJIANG

Serves: 4–6

120g (4¼oz) Chinese celery (see page 14)
40g (1½oz) spring onions (scallions)
60g (2oz) doubanjiang (spicy fermented broad bean paste)
20ml (4 tsp) rice vinegar
30g (2 tbsp) granulated sugar

For seasoning, coating and frying the chicken
800g (1lb 12oz) boneless chicken thighs
coarse salt flakes, as necessary
3–4 peeled garlic cloves
1 small chunk of peeled ginger
2 tsp Sichuan peppercorns
30ml (2 tbsp) rice wine
5g (1 tsp) granulated sugar
100g (3½oz) coating mix made with tapioca flour (see page 162)
about 50ml (generous 3 tbsp) iced water
120g (4¼oz) tapioca flour
765ml (3⅓ cups) cooking oil

Doubanjiang is essential to Sichuan cuisine, where it's used in all kinds of dishes you might be familiar with, including Mapo Tofu, twice-cooked pork, and the mung bean noodle dish known as 'ants climbing a tree'. It's distinctively and powerfully flavourful and makes a delicious coating for fried chicken.

Butterfly the chicken thighs (see page 20), cut them into 3cm (1¼in) chunks and put them in a bowl. Weigh the chicken, then multiply the amount by 0.01 – this is the amount of salt you need. Sprinkle the salt over the chicken and mix well.

Use a fine grater – preferably a ceramic oroshigane, see page 17 – to grate the garlic and ginger. Weigh out 10g (⅓oz) of each, then put them in the bowl with the chicken. Toast the Sichuan peppercorns by putting them in an unoiled frying pan (skillet) and heating it over a medium heat. Shake the pan constantly until the peppercorns are toasted. Cool the peppercorns, grind them to a rough powder, then add them to the chicken along with the rice wine and sugar. Mix well, then marinate at room temperature for 30 minutes–2 hours.

Separate the leaves from the Chinese celery stalks. Set aside the leaves to use as a garnish and tear the stalks into 5cm (2in) pieces. Cut the spring onions into 2.5cm (1in) lengths. Mix the doubanjiang with the vinegar, sugar and 30ml (2 tbsp) water.

Add the coating mix and the iced water to the bowl of chicken and mix well to create a batter that coats the pieces lightly and evenly. If necessary, adjust the consistency by mixing in more iced water.

Dredge the battered chicken in the tapioca flour, shake off the excess, then lay the pieces on a cooling rack placed over a tray. Leave them to air-dry for at least 10 minutes, then dredge them again.

Pour 750ml (3¼ cups) cooking oil into a pan, preferably a medium wok, set over a medium heat. Fry the chicken at 160°C (320°F) in four or five batches. Fry for 3–4 minutes, then drain on the rack placed over the tray. After frying the last batch, fry the chicken again, this time at 170°C (340°F) for about 1½ minutes.

Pour 15ml (1 tablespoon) oil into a large wok and place over a high heat. Add the celery and spring onions and stir-fry until the spring onions are bright green. Remove from the wok.

Pour the doubanjiang mixture into the wok and bring to the boil over a medium–low heat. Add the chicken and mix until the pieces are coated with the sauce. Add the celery and spring onions back into the wok, then stir constantly until the coating is dry and clings to the chicken. Transfer to a serving platter and garnish with the celery leaves.

BONELESS
BREASTS

〜〜〜〜〜〜〜〜〜〜

I actually dreaded writing this chapter. I have never – not once – eaten a chicken breast dish where I didn't think it would be so much better with dark meat. But I was determined to make chicken breast that I liked. And I have succeeded.

The trick is in not overcooking the chicken. In fact, I take it out of the hot oil when it is slightly undercooked and let the residual heat finish cooking it. With the smaller pieces of chicken, it's cooked for as little as 30 seconds, then rested for about 5 minutes before being fried a second time for 30 seconds. Slightly undercooking it, and also pre-salting the meat for at least 30 minutes results in chicken breast that even I will happily eat.

With chicken breast, it is especially important that the pieces be as evenly thick as possible, and very close to the same size. Butterfly the breasts (see page 20) and take care when cutting them. If the pieces are too large or too small, it will change the cooking time, which might result in under- or overcooked chicken.

TAIWANESE NIGHT MARKET CHICKEN

~~~~~~~~~~~~~~~~~~~~~~~~~~~~~

Serves: 4–6

800g (1lb 12oz) boneless chicken breast
coarse salt flakes, as necessary
30g (1oz) chunk of peeled ginger
  (use as necessary)
5–8 peeled garlic cloves (use as necessary)
20ml (4 tsp) soy sauce
  (all-purpose Kikkoman or your
  favourite brand)
20ml (4 tsp) rice wine
5g (1 tsp) granulated sugar
1½ tsp finely ground white pepper
1 tsp five-spice powder
1½ tsp Tianjin chilli powder
100g (3½oz) coating mix made with sweet
  potato flour (see page 162)
about 50ml (generous 3 tbsp) iced water
about 120g (4¼oz) sweet potato flour
750ml (3¼ cups) cooking oil
60g (2oz) holy basil leaves (see note)

For the seasoning salt

5g (1 tsp) coarse salt flakes
1½ tsp granulated sugar
1–1½ tsp Tianjin chilli powder
1 tsp finely ground white pepper
¾ tsp five-spice powder
½ tsp paprika

Note

*Do not wash the basil leaves before using
them. Just take them out of any packaging and
lay them out to dry on a dish towel. If there's
moisture on them when you fry them, the oil will
splatter excessively.*

**One of my favourite things to do whenever I visit Taipei is to go to the
night markets for a few hours of snacking. We take our time walking
through the crowd, occasionally stopping for a drink or a shaved ice,
between munching on savoury snacks... there's so much choice, and
it's all so good. There's always a queue at the fried chicken vendor,
which sells large or even extra-large flattened chicken breasts. They
won't cut it for you, explaining that it will make the juices escape.
My preference is for the fried chicken nuggets, which, like the large
breasts, are dusted with a sweet-savoury-spicy seasoned salt and
served with fried basil leaves.**

Butterfly the chicken breasts (see page 20), cut them into 4cm (1½in) chunks, then
put them in a bowl. Weigh the chicken, then multiply the amount by 0.01 – this is
the amount of salt you need. Add the salt, mix well and leave for 30 minutes.

Use a fine grater – preferably a ceramic oroshigane, see page 17 – to grate
the ginger and garlic to a smooth paste, then weigh out 20g (¾oz) of each.
Mix the ginger and garlic with the soy sauce, rice wine, sugar, white pepper,
five-spice and chilli powders. Add this to the chicken and mix well, then leave
to marinate at room temperature for at least 1 hour.

Mix together all the ingredients for the seasoning salt. Set aside.

Sprinkle the coating mix over the chicken and add the iced water to create
a batter that coats the pieces lightly and evenly. If necessary, mix in more iced
water to adjust the consistency.

Dredge the battered chicken pieces in the sweet potato flour, shake off the
excess, then lay them on a cooling rack placed over a tray.

Pour the cooking oil into a pan, preferably a medium wok, set over a medium
heat. Fry the basil leaves at 160°C (320°F) until translucent. Drain them on paper
towels. Fry the chicken at 160°C (320°F) in four or five batches. Fry each batch
for 1 minute, then drain on the cooling rack placed over the tray. Let the pieces
rest for 5 minutes, then fry them a second time at 170°C (340°F) for 1 minute. As
soon as each batch has fried a second time, drain it briefly, then put the pieces
in a metal bowl. Sprinkle lightly with some of the seasoning salt and mix and
toss the pieces so they are evenly seasoned. Put the pieces on the rack to finish
cooling, then repeat the process with each batch of chicken.

Pile the chicken pieces on a serving plate and add the fried basil leaves. Serve
the remaining seasoning salt on the side, for diners to add to taste.

CHICKEN NANBAN

~~~~~~~~~~~~~~~~~~~~~~~~~~~~~~~~~~~~ Serves: 4–6

800g (1lb 12oz) boneless chicken breast
coarse salt flakes, as necessary
30ml (2 tbsp) soy sauce
    (all-purpose Kikkoman or your
    favourite brand)
20ml (4 tsp) sake
5g (1 tsp) granulated sugar
1 tsp finely ground white pepper
100g (3½oz) coating mix made with potato
    or sweet potato flour (see page 162)
about 40ml (2 tbsp + 2 tsp) iced water
about 120g (4¼oz) potato or sweet
    potato flour
750ml (3¼ cups) cooking oil

For the nanban sauce
60ml (¼ cup) soy sauce
    (all-purpose Kikkoman or your
    favourite brand)
60ml (¼ cup) sake
60ml (¼ cup) mirin
30g (2 tbsp) granulated sugar
30g (2 tbsp) honey
60ml (¼ cup) rice vinegar

For the tartare sauce
2 eggs
60g (2oz) peeled onion
40–60g (1½–2oz) cornichons or gherkins
180g (6¼oz) Kewpie mayonnaise (see note)
½ tsp medium-grind black pepper,
    or more to taste

Note
*For the right flavour, it's important to use
Kewpie mayonnaise (a Japanese brand) for
the tartare sauce.*

**This is one of my favourite ways to eat chicken breast – it's yoshoku
(Western-influenced Japanese food) at its best. It sounds like an
unlikely combination: fried chicken dunked into a light sauce, then
served with tartare sauce, a condiment that, in the west, is usually
an accompaniment to seafood. I often serve this with Japanese rice,
shredded cabbage and takuan (pickled radish) or cucumber pickles.**

Butterfly the chicken breasts (see page 20), cut them into 3cm (1¼in) chunks
and put them in a bowl. Weigh the chicken, then multiply the amount by 0.01
– this is the amount of salt you need. Add the salt, mix well and leave for at least
30 minutes. Add the soy sauce, sake, sugar and white pepper to the chicken,
mix well and marinate at room temperature for at least 1 hour.

While the chicken is marinating, make the tartare sauce. Put the eggs in a pan
and add water to cover by 1cm (½in). Place over a medium heat, then bring to
the boil. Cover the pan with the lid, turn off the heat and leave for 12 minutes.
Drain off the water, then transfer the eggs to a bowl filled with iced water and
leave to cool. Crack the eggs and remove the shells.

Finely mince the onion, then put the pieces in a bowl of iced water and leave for
a few minutes. (This makes the onion taste sweeter.) Drain off the water, then dry
the onion with paper towels. Cut the cornichons into small dice and chop the
eggs. Mix the eggs, onion and cornichons with the Kewpie mayonnaise and add
the black pepper. Put the tartare sauce into a bowl and set aside.

To make the nanban sauce, pour the soy sauce, sake, mirin, sugar and honey into
a saucepan and place it on the stove top, but do not turn on the heat.

Add the coating mix and the iced water to the bowl of chicken and mix well to
create a batter that coats the pieces lightly and evenly. If necessary, adjust the
consistency by mixing in more iced water.

Dredge the battered chicken pieces in the potato or sweet potato flour, shake
off the excess and lay them on a cooling rack placed over a tray.

Pour the cooking oil into a pan, preferably a medium wok, set over a medium
heat. Fry the chicken at 160°C (320°F) in four or five batches. Fry the chicken for
45 seconds, then drain on the rack. Let the pieces rest for 5 minutes, then fry
them a second time at 170°C (340°F) for 45 seconds.

Bring the nanban sauce to the boil over a medium heat and simmer for
1 minute. Add the vinegar and simmer for 30 seconds, then turn off the heat.
Put half of the fried chicken into a bowl and add half the nanban sauce. Toss the
pieces in the bowl so they are lightly coated with the sauce. Transfer to a serving
dish, then repeat with the remaining chicken and sauce.

Spoon some of the tartare sauce over the chicken and serve the rest on the side.

CHICKEN NUGGETS WITH SAMBAL BELACAN & COCONUT MILK

Serves: 4–6

800g (1lb 12oz) boneless chicken breast
coarse salt flakes, as necessary
120g (4¼oz) sambal belacan (see intro)
5g (1 tsp) granulated sugar
1–2 tsp Tianjin chilli powder
20ml (4 tsp) fresh lime juice
60ml (¼ cup) canned coconut milk
about 100g (3½oz) coating mix
  (see page 162)
about 120g (4¼oz) potato, sweet potato or
  tapioca flour
750ml (3¼ cups) cooking oil
fresh limes (calamansi or Thai), to garnish

I love sambal belacan, a spicy, pungent condiment that has belacan – fermented shrimp paste – as its base. In the past, when I travelled more, I would usually pick up packets of it from small producers on my trips to Malaysia or Singapore, to store in the fridge or freezer. These days, I buy commercially produced jars of it.

This recipe calls for fresh lime juice and fresh limes for the garnish. Calamansi limes – tiny, very fragrant and juicy citrus – are the best, but Thai limes are fine, too.

Butterfly the chicken breasts (see page 20), cut them into 2.5cm (1in) chunks and put them in a bowl. Weigh the chicken, then multiply the amount by 0.01 – this is the amount of salt you need. Add the salt, mix well and leave for at least 30 minutes.

Put the sambal belacan into a bowl and stir in the sugar and chilli powder. Mix in the lime juice, then slowly stir in the coconut milk. Pour this mixture over the chicken and leave to marinate at room temperature for 2–3 hours.

Sprinkle the coating mix over the chicken, adding enough to create a batter that coats the pieces lightly and evenly. If necessary, adjust the consistency by mixing in some iced water. Dredge the battered chicken pieces in the potato, sweet potato or tapioca flour, shake off the excess, then lay them on a cooling rack placed over a tray. Leave to air-dry for at least 10 minutes.

Pour the cooking oil into a pan, preferably a medium wok, set over a medium heat. Fry the chicken at 160°C (320°F) in four or five batches. Fry the chicken for 30 seconds, then drain on the rack. Let the pieces rest for 5 minutes, then fry them a second time at 170°C (340°F) for 30 seconds.

Pile the nuggets into a bowl or plate and garnish with the limes. If using calamansi limes, just cut off the top to expose the bright orange flesh; for Thai limes, cut them as instructed on page 15.

BONELESS BREASTS

CHICKEN SALAD WITH MOUTH-WATERING DRESSING

Serves: 4

400g (14oz) boneless chicken breast

coarse salt flakes, as necessary

½ tsp finely ground white pepper

750ml (3¼ cups) cooking oil

about 60g (2oz) potato or sweet
  potato flour

1–2 eggs

about 60g (2oz) panko breadcrumbs

For the dressing

2 tsp Sichuan peppercorns (use to taste)

1–2 peeled garlic cloves

1–2 thin slices of peeled ginger

60ml (¼ cup) soy sauce
  (all-purpose Kikkoman or your
  favourite brand)

20ml (4 tsp) rice vinegar or Chinese
  brown vinegar

10g (2 tsp) granulated sugar

15ml (1 tbsp) sesame oil

15ml (1 tbsp) Chinese chilli oil, or to taste

½ tsp toasted sesame seeds, plus extra for
  sprinkling

For the salad

400g (14oz) white cabbage

150g (5½oz) Chinese celery (see page 14)

30g (1oz) fresh coriander (cilantro) leaves,
  stems and roots (see page 14)

2 Asian cucumbers, about 120g
  (4¼oz) each

2 spring onions (scallions)

10g (⅓oz) thin rice vermicelli

90g (3oz) roasted peanuts

**The dressing for this salad gets its evocative name because it's said
to be so delicious it makes your mouth water. It's often served with
poached chicken, but I love it with chicken salad that has lots of
flavours and textures from cabbage, Chinese celery, roasted peanuts
and fried rice vermicelli.**

Butterfly the chicken breasts (see page 20), then lay each one on a large
piece of clingfilm (plastic wrap) and cover with another piece of clingfilm. Use
the flat side of a metal meat mallet to pound the breast to flatten it slightly
– you don't want it to be too thin. After pounding all the breasts, cut them into
pieces weighing 70–80g (2½–2¾oz) each. Weigh the chicken, then multiply the
amount by 0.015 – this is the amount of salt you need. Put the chicken in a bowl,
add the salt and pepper, mix well and leave for at least 30 minutes.

To prepare the dressing, toast the Sichuan peppercorns in a dry (unoiled) frying
pan (skillet) placed over a medium heat. Shake the pan almost constantly so you
don't burn the peppercorns. Cool briefly, then grind them to a rough powder.
Finely mince the garlic and ginger.

In a bowl, whisk the soy sauce with the vinegar and sugar until the sugar is
dissolved. Whisk in the sesame and chilli oils, then add the garlic, ginger, toasted
sesame seeds and 1 teaspoon of the ground Sichuan pepper. Taste the dressing
and add more Sichuan pepper and chilli oil, if you like.

For the salad, finely shred the cabbage. Separate the leaves from the stalks of
the Chinese celery. Tear the stalks into 5cm (2in) lengths. Separate the leaves
from the stems and roots of the fresh coriander. Finely mince the roots and
stems. Cut the cucumbers in half lengthways, then slice them on the diagonal
into 5mm (¼in) pieces. Thinly slice the spring onions.

Pour the cooking oil into a 28cm (11¼in) frying pan, preferably cast iron, set over
a medium heat. Add the rice vermicelli and fry in batches at 170°C (340°F) until
they puff up and turn white. Drain on paper towels.

Put the potato or sweet potato flour in a shallow dish. Whisk the eggs in another
shallow dish and put the panko in a third dish. Dredge the chicken pieces in
the flour and shake off the excess, then dip in the egg. Dredge in the panko,
pressing firmly so that the breadcrumbs adhere. Lay the pieces on a cooling
rack placed over a tray.

Fry the chicken fillets in batches at 170°C (340°F) for about 3–3½ minutes,
then drain on a cooling rack placed over a tray.

To assemble the salad, put the cabbage, Chinese celery stalks, coriander stems/roots and cucumbers in a large bowl and add about 60ml (¼ cup) of the dressing. Mix with your hands to lightly coat the vegetables. Divide the greens between four plates. Slice the chicken into strips and divide them between the plates, then top each portion with some of the rice noodles. Scatter peanuts and the spring onions on top, add the celery and coriander leaves, then drizzle each portion with some of the dressing and sprinkle with sesame seeds. Serve the remaining dressing on the side.

LEMON CHICKEN

~~~~~~

Serves: 4–6

800g (1lb 12oz) boneless chicken breast
coarse salt flakes, as necessary
20ml (4 tsp) soy sauce
    (all-purpose Kikkoman or your
    favourite brand)
20ml (4 tsp) rice wine
½ tsp finely ground white pepper
15g (½oz) cornflour (cornstarch)
about 120g (4¼oz) potato or sweet
    potato flour
2–3 eggs
about 120g (4¼oz) panko breadcrumbs
750ml (3¼ cups) cooking oil

For the sauce
finely grated zest of 2 lemons
90–120ml (6 tbsp–½ cup) fresh lemon juice
60g (¼ cup) granulated sugar
½ tsp coarse salt flakes
1 tsp sesame oil
10g (⅓oz) cornflour (cornstarch)
sesame seeds, for sprinkling
lemon slices, to garnish

In the USA, I have eaten absolutely horrendous versions of lemon chicken. One had a sauce that I am absolutely convinced was made from lemon jelly (jello) that was melted, then diluted with food colouring – it was fluorescent yellow and disgustingly sweet. My ideal lemon chicken has moist meat and a light, tart sauce that tastes of fresh lemon, so that's what I made here.

Butterfly the chicken breasts (see page 20), then lay each one on a large piece of clingfilm (plastic wrap) and cover with another piece of clingfilm. Use the flat side of a metal meat mallet to pound the breast to flatten it slightly – you don't want it to be too thin. After pounding all the breasts, cut them into pieces weighing about 60g (2oz) each. Weigh the chicken, then multiply the amount by 0.015 – this is the amount of salt you need. Put the chicken in a bowl, add the salt, mix well and leave for at least 30 minutes.

Add the soy sauce, rice wine, white pepper and cornflour to the chicken, then mix well and set aside for about 30 minutes.

Put the potato or sweet potato flour in a shallow dish. Whisk the eggs in another shallow dish and put the panko in a third dish. Dredge the chicken fillets in the flour and shake off the excess, then dip in the egg. Dredge in the panko, pressing firmly so that the breadcrumbs adhere. Lay the pieces on a cooling rack placed over a tray.

Pour the cooking oil into a 28cm (11¼in) frying pan (skillet), preferably cast iron, set over a medium heat, filling it about halfway. Fry the chicken fillets in batches for about 2½–3 minutes at 170°C (340°F), then drain on the rack placed over the tray.

To make the sauce, put the lemon zest, lemon juice, sugar, salt and sesame oil into a small pan and place over a medium heat. In a small bowl, stir the cornflour with 40ml (2 tbsp + 2 tsp) water. When the lemon mixture comes to the boil, drizzle in the cornflour mixture, stirring the sauce constantly. Stir in 30ml (2 tablespoons) of hot oil (from frying the chicken) and simmer the ingredients. Add about 60ml (¼ cup) hot water, to thin out the sauce as necessary – it should lightly coat a spoon. Pour the sauce into a serving bowl and sprinkle with sesame seeds.

Slice the chicken into pieces about 1.25cm (½in) wide, then put on a plate, garnish with lemon slices and serve the sauce on the side.

COCONUT MILK & CURRY POWDER NUGGETS

Serves: 4–6

800g (1lb 12oz) boneless chicken breast

coarse salt flakes, as necessary

20g (¾oz) lemongrass (the lower
    8cm/3¼in of 2 stalks)

10g (⅓oz) fresh galangal

40g (1½oz) peeled shallots

20g (¾oz) peeled garlic cloves

15g (1 tbsp) granulated sugar

1 tsp Tianjin chilli powder

1 tsp ground turmeric

2 tsp curry powder

180ml (¾ cup) canned coconut milk

about 150g (5½oz) coating mix
    (see page 162)

about 120g (4¼oz) potato, sweet potato or
    tapioca flour

750ml (3¼ cups) cooking oil

toasted, unsweetened coconut shreds,
    for sprinkling

fried shallots, for sprinkling

Curry powder is an ingredient that often people associate with Indian cooking, although many traditional Indian cooks would never use it, and instead, would make specific spice blends to suit specific dishes. I treat it as I would any spice and use it in combination with other seasonings on my shelves. In this dish, the strong flavour of curry powder is balanced by the sweetness of coconut milk. If you don't want the marinade to stain your hand when you mix the ingredients, wear a rubber or plastic glove.

Butterfly the chicken breasts (see page 20), cut them into 3cm (1¼in) chunks and put them in a bowl. Weigh the chicken, then multiply the amount by 0.015 – this is the amount of salt you need. Add the salt, mix well and leave for at least 30 minutes.

Use a metal meat mallet to bash the lower 8cm (3¼in) of the stalks of lemongrass. Slice the stalks as thinly as possible and weigh out 20g (¾oz). Thinly slice the galangal and chop the shallots and garlic. Put these ingredients in a mortar and pound to a rough paste, then scrape into a bowl. Stir in the sugar, chilli powder, turmeric, curry powder and coconut milk. Add this to the chicken, mix well and marinate at room temperature for 2–3 hours.

Sprinkle the coating mix over the chicken to create a batter that coats the pieces lightly and evenly. If necessary, adjust the consistency by adding more coating mix or some iced water. Dredge the battered pieces in the potato, sweet potato or tapioca flour, shake off the excess, then lay the pieces on a cooling rack placed over a tray.

Pour the cooking oil into a pan, preferably a medium wok, set over a medium heat. Fry the chicken at 160°C (320°F) in four or five batches. Fry the chicken for 45 seconds, then drain on the rack. Let the pieces rest for 5 minutes, then fry them a second time at 170°C (340°F) for 45 seconds.

Put the chicken pieces on a plate and scatter with the coconut and fried shallots, to serve.

PAPER-WRAPPED CHICKEN

Serves: 4–6

800g (1lb 12oz) boneless chicken breast
coarse salt flakes, as necessary
30g (1oz) peeled ginger
60g (2oz) spring onions (scallions)
40g (2 tbsp + 2 tsp) oyster sauce
20ml (4 tsp) soy sauce
  (all-purpose Kikkoman or your
  favourite brand)
15ml (1 tbsp) rice wine
5ml (1 tsp) sesame oil
5g (1 tsp) granulated sugar
5g (1 tsp) coarse salt flakes
½ tsp finely ground white pepper
1 tbsp cornflour (cornstarch)
750ml (3¼ cups) cooking oil

People often think of Chinese paper-wrapped chicken as a restaurant dish for tourists, but my first taste of it was at the house of my Ah Ma (paternal grandmother). She was an excellent cook who, with the help of my father – her eldest son – and later, me, would cook for about 15–20 family members every Saturday night, and about the same number every Sunday lunch. Her version of this dish used aluminium foil, but I like to use parchment paper. The parchment (or foil, if you prefer) prevents the chicken from coming into direct contact with the oil, so it stays tender, and at the same time, the ingredients steam in the tightly sealed parcel, which locks in the moisture and flavour.

Butterfly the chicken breasts (see page 20), cut them into 1.5cm (⅝in) pieces and put them in a bowl. Weigh the chicken, then multiply the amount by 0.01 – this is the amount of salt you need. Add the salt, mix well and leave for at least 30 minutes.

Finely julienne the ginger and cut the spring onions into 2.5cm (1in) lengths. Add the oyster sauce, soy sauce, rice wine, sesame oil, sugar, salt, pepper and cornflour to the chicken. Mix well, then stir in the ginger and spring onions. Leave to marinate at room temperature for 1–2 hours, mixing occasionally.

Cut 28–32 pieces of parchment paper that are 15cm (6in) square. Working with several squares at a time, crumble the parchment into a ball, then smooth it out – this makes the paper less stiff and therefore easier to fold tightly.

Line up four to eight squares of parchment on the work surface (depending on space), with a corner of each one pointing at you. Place some of the chicken, ginger and spring onions in an 8cm (3¼in) wide strip on each square, about 7cm (2¾in) above the bottom corner. Fold the bottom corner up and over the chicken. Fold the paper (with the chicken) up just past the midpoint of the square, then press your palms on the sides of the filling, to compress it back to 8cm (3¼in). Fold both sides of the paper towards the centre so they overlap, then fold up the paper once more towards the far corner. Tuck the top corner tightly into the fold between the main part of the paper and the two folded-in side pieces of parchment, then press with the palm of your hand to slightly flatten the 'envelope'. Lay the filled parcels on a tray and repeat with the remaining chicken and paper.

Pour the cooking oil into a pan, preferably a medium wok, set over a medium heat. Fry the chicken pieces in batches at 175°C (347°F) for about 3 minutes. Take the parcels out of the oil, then put them seam-side down – so the oil can run out – on a cooling rack placed over a tray.

Let your guests unwrap the parcels at the table.

JAPANESE CHICKEN NUGGETS

Serves: 4–6

800g (1lb 12oz) boneless chicken breast

coarse salt flakes, as necessary

25g (1oz) peeled garlic cloves

finely grated zest of 1 lemon

60ml (¼ cup) fresh lemon juice

½ tsp finely ground white pepper

about 100g (3½oz) coating mix made from
 potato flour (see page 162)

2 large eggs

about 150g (5½oz) panko breadcrumbs

25g (1oz) furikake (see intro)

1 tbsp gochugaru (Korean chilli flakes)

4 tsp black and white sesame seeds

750ml (3¼ cups) cooking oil

The chicken breast for this dish is seasoned with lemon zest and lemon juice, which gives the meat a fresh, light, zingy flavour. Serve the chicken with bowls of Japanese rice, some finely shredded cabbage, and a big blob of Kewpie mayonnaise sprinkled with shichimi togarashi (Japanese seven spice).

Furikake – also known as Japanese rice sprinkles – come in many flavours. I like the type with a little chilli powder, but pick your own favourite.

Butterfly the chicken breasts (see page 20), cut them into 4cm (1½in) chunks and put them in a bowl. Weigh the chicken, then multiply the amount by 0.015 – this is the amount of salt you need. Add the salt, mix well and leave for at least 30 minutes.

Mince the garlic and add it to the chicken, along with the lemon zest, lemon juice and pepper. Marinate for no longer than 2 hours at room temperature.

Put the coating mix in a shallow dish. Whisk the eggs and put them in another shallow dish. In a third dish, mix the panko with the furikake, gochugaru and sesame seeds. Dredge the chicken pieces in the coating mix, then dip in the beaten egg. Dredge in the panko, pressing firmly so that the breadcrumbs adhere. Lay the pieces on a cooling rack placed over a tray.

Pour the cooking oil into a pan, preferably a medium wok, set over a medium heat. Fry the chicken at 160°C (320°F) in three or four batches. Fry for 2 minutes, then drain the nuggets on the rack. There's no need for a second frying.

THAI-FLAVOURED CHICKEN WITH LEMONGRASS & MINT

Serves: 4–6

8–12 red bird's-eye chillies

90g (3oz) peeled shallots

50g (1¾oz) lemongrass (the lower 8cm/3¼in of 4–5 stalks)

40ml (2 tbsp + 2 tsp) fish sauce

30g (2 tbsp) sugar – preferably muscovado or palm sugar

50ml (generous 3 tbsp) fresh lime juice

butterhead or romaine lettuce leaves

40g (1½oz) fresh mint leaves

20g (¾oz) fresh coriander (cilantro) leaves

80g (2¾oz) roasted salted cashews or peanuts

For coating and frying the chicken

600g (1lb 5oz) boneless chicken breast

coarse salt flakes, as necessary

1 tsp finely ground white pepper

80g (2¾oz) coating mix (see page 162)

about 60ml (¼ cup) iced water

about 90g (3oz) potato, sweet potato or tapioca flour

750ml (3¼ cups) cooking oil

I first made this dish with leftover chicken – because when you're testing fried chicken recipes every day, you end up with a lot of leftovers. It was good, but then I made it again with freshly fried chicken, and it was even better. I like to pretend that it's a salad because it does have lettuce in it, but it's not what most people consider salad.

Butterfly the chicken breasts (see page 20), cut them into 3cm (1¼in) chunks and put them in a bowl. Weigh the chicken, then multiply the amount by 0.01 – this is the amount of salt you need. Add the salt and pepper to the chicken, mix well, then leave for at least 30 minutes.

Slice the chillies into thin rings, shaking out and discarding the seeds as you go. Halve the shallots, then thinly slice them. Use a metal meat mallet to bash the lower 8cm (3¼in) of the lemongrass stalks, then slice them as thinly as possible before weighing out 50g (1¾oz). Stir the fish sauce with the sugar until dissolved, then add the lime juice. Taste for seasonings and adjust, if necessary. Set aside.

Sprinkle the coating mix over the chicken and add the iced water. Mix to form a thin batter that lightly coats the chicken. If necessary, adjust the consistency by adding more iced water.

Dredge the battered chicken in the potato, sweet potato or tapioca flour, then lay the pieces on a cooling rack placed over a tray.

Pour the cooking oil into a pan, preferably a medium wok, set over a medium heat. Fry the chicken at 160°C (320°F) in four or five batches. Fry for 45 seconds, then drain on the rack. Let the pieces rest for 5 minutes, then fry them again at 170°C (340°F) for 45 seconds.

Line a serving plate (or four to six individual plates) with lettuce leaves. Put the chillies, shallots, lemongrass, and the mint and coriander leaves in a bowl and add the fish sauce mixture. Mix well, then add the chicken and half the cashews or peanuts and mix again so the ingredients are lightly coated.

Pile the ingredients onto the plate(s) and scatter with the remaining cashews or peanuts.

MALA NUGGETS

Serves: 4–6

800g (1lb 12oz) boneless chicken breast
coarse salt flakes, as necessary
2 tbsp Sichuan peppercorns
  (use as necessary)
20ml (4 tsp) rice wine
2 tsp Tianjin chilli powder
1½ tsp granulated sugar
100g (3½oz) coating mix, preferably made
  from tapioca flour (see page 162)
about 50ml (generous 3 tbsp) iced water
120g (4¼oz) tapioca flour
750ml (3¼ cups) cooking oil

The 'ma' in 'mala' refers to the numbing sensation of Sichuan peppercorns, while the 'la' refers to the chilli hotness from the Tianjin chillies. When combined, they are the very essence of Sichuanese cuisine.

Butterfly the chicken breasts (see page 20), cut them into 2.5cm (1in) chunks and put them in a bowl. Weigh the chicken, then multiply the amount by 0.01 – this is the amount of salt you need. Sprinkle the salt over the chicken and mix well, then leave for at least 30 minutes.

Put the Sichuan peppercorns in an unoiled frying pan (skillet) placed over a medium heat and stir them almost constantly until they are fragrant and toasted. Cool them slightly, then grind them to a fine powder.

Add the rice wine to the chicken pieces, along with 1 tablespoon of the ground Sichuan pepper, 1½ teaspoons of the Tianjin chilli powder and the sugar. Mix well and marinate at room temperature for at least 1 hour.

Mix the coating mix with 1½ teaspoons of ground Sichuan pepper and the remaining ½ teaspoon of Tianjin chilli. Sprinkle this over the chicken, then add the iced water and mix to create a batter that coats the pieces lightly and evenly. If necessary, adjust the consistency by mixing in a little more iced water. Dredge the battered chicken in the tapioca flour and lay the pieces on a cooling rack placed over a tray.

Pour the cooking oil into a pan, preferably a medium wok, set over a medium heat. Fry the chicken at 160°C (320°F) in four or five batches. Fry for 30 seconds, then drain on the rack. Let the pieces rest for 5 minutes, then fry them again at 170°C (340°F) for 30 seconds.

Pile the pieces onto a plate, then serve.

BONE-IN THIGHS, DRUMSTICKS & WHOLE BIRDS

When someone mentions fried chicken, the bone-in drumsticks and thighs are the first parts that I think of because they featured so prominently when I was growing up in California. We always had fried chicken legs when we went to the beach, often accompanied by Umeboshi Onigiri (rice balls with salted plums) and Hawaiian Mac (macaroni) Salad (page 171) made by my Japanese-Hawaiian aunt. We often took chicken on car road trips because it's easy to eat out of hand. And my Ah Ma (maternal grandmother), who had a repertoire of about six non-Chinese dishes (her Chinese repertoire was vast) made delicious fried chicken, which she served with spaghetti with tomato sauce. I didn't realize until I'd moved away from home that fried chicken and spaghetti is considered an unusual pairing.

The frying times are for fairly small drumsticks and thighs that weigh between 120–150g (4¼–5½oz). If your chicken pieces are larger, you'll need to cook them for longer.

If you've refrigerated the chicken to marinate it, be sure to let it come to room temperature before frying it.

CHINESE-AMERICAN DELI FRIED CHICKEN

Serves: 4–6

8–10 bone-in drumsticks and/or thighs, about 120–150g (4¼–5½oz) each

6–10 peeled garlic cloves

30g (1oz) chunk of peeled ginger

120ml (½ cup) soy sauce (all-purpose Kikkoman or your favourite brand)

60ml (¼ cup) rice wine

10g (2 tsp) granulated sugar

1 tsp finely ground white pepper

about 100g (3½oz) coating mix (see page 162)

about 150g (5½oz) potato, sweet potato or tapioca flour

about 750ml (3¼ cups) cooking oil

This is my version of the fried chicken we ate several times a year (along with my dad's Chow Mein) at our village Kow Kong Benevolent Association gatherings in southern California. The uncle who made the chicken used only drumsticks and thighs because they were the pieces that we preferred – if anyone liked the breast meat, we weren't aware of it! I use the marinade as the liquid to stir into the coating mix, instead of using water; this way, the batter has a lot more flavour.

Double slash the chicken pieces on both sides, cutting all the way to the bone. Lightly crush the garlic cloves, then roughly chop them. Bash the ginger with a meat mallet, then roughly chop it. Put the soy sauce and rice wine in a bowl, add the sugar and stir to dissolve. Mix in the garlic, ginger and white pepper. Add the chicken pieces to the bowl and mix well, then marinate in the fridge for at least 6 hours, mixing occasionally.

Transfer the chicken pieces to a clean bowl. Pour 90ml (6 tablespoons) of the marinade through a sieve (strainer) into the bowl; discard the solids.

Add 100g (3½oz) coating mix to the bowl with the chicken and mix well to create a batter that coats the chicken pieces lightly and evenly. If necessary, add more coating mix or marinade to adjust the consistency. Dredge the battered chicken pieces in the potato, sweet potato or tapioca flour. Shake off the excess flour, then lay the chicken pieces on a cooling rack placed over a tray. Leave them to air-dry for at least 10 minutes.

Pour cooking oil into a 28cm (11¼in) frying pan (skillet), preferably cast iron, to fill it about halfway. Heat the oil, then fry the chicken in two batches at 150–160°C (300–320°F). Fry the chicken for 12–15 minutes, turning over the pieces as necessary. Take the chicken out of the pan and drain on the rack placed over the tray. Let the chicken rest for at least 10 minutes.

Heat the oil again, then fry the chicken at 170°C (340°F) for 2 minutes, turning over the pieces once. Drain the chicken on the rack.

Serve the chicken warm or at room temperature.

AYAM GORENG BEREMPAH

~~~~~~ **Serves: 4–6**

10–12 bone-in drumsticks and/or thighs, about 120–150g (4¼–5½oz) each
coarse sea salt flakes, as necessary
1 tsp finely ground white pepper
15g (1 tbsp) granulated sugar
about 750ml (3¼ cups) cooking oil

For the spice paste
20g (¾oz) lemongrass (the lower 8cm/3¼in of 2 stalks)
10g (⅓oz) fresh turmeric
30g (1oz) peeled garlic cloves
120g (4¼oz) peeled red onion
15g (½oz) fresh galangal
20g (¾oz) peeled ginger
6 candlenuts or macadamia nuts
75g (5 tbsp) tamarind paste
1½ tbsp curry powder
1½ tbsp Tianjin chilli powder
1½ tbsp ground cumin
1 tbsp ground coriander
1 tbsp ground fennel
20–25g (4–5 tsp) granulated sugar
10g (2 tsp) coarse salt flakes
15g (½oz) cornflour (cornstarch)
15g (½oz) glutinous rice flour
8 x 10cm (4in) stalks of fresh curry leaves

This delicious, complexly spiced fried chicken is my adaptation of a recipe given to me by my friend Jonathan, who, in turn, modified his version from a YouTube video by Malaysian cook, K L Liew. The list of ingredients is long, but the preparation isn't difficult: you prepare a spice paste, rub it into the meat, then fry it the next day. There is a rather unusual step in the end, where you fry the spice paste until it forms crisp, intensely flavourful crumbs that are delicious with steamed rice.

This fried chicken is unusual in that it doesn't have much of a starch coating – just a scant amount of cornflour (cornstarch) and glutinous rice flour are mixed into the marinade. The chicken is fried only once – it's not double fried.

Double slash the chicken pieces on both sides, cutting all the way to the bone, and put in a bowl. Weigh the chicken, then multiply the amount by 0.005 – this is the amount of salt you need. Sprinkle the chicken with the salt, pepper and sugar. Mix well, then set aside while preparing the other ingredients.

Use a metal meat mallet to bash the length of the lemongrass stalks, then thinly slice them before weighing out 20g (4 teaspoons). Use a teaspoon to scrape the skin from the turmeric. Roughly chop the garlic, red onion, turmeric, galangal and ginger. Put all of these ingredients in a blender (preferably a high-speed blender) and add the nuts, the tamarind paste and 30ml (2 tablespoons) water. Blend until the ingredients are as smooth as possible; if necessary, add in a little more water.

Put the paste in a bowl and add the curry powder, chilli powder, cumin, coriander, fennel, 20g (4 teaspoons) of the sugar and the salt. Taste the mixture – it should be spicy but balanced. If necessary, add a little more sugar. Rub the spice paste into the chicken, coating it well (wear a rubber glove, or your hand will smell of the paste). Cover the bowl, then leave to marinate in the fridge for at least 8 hours.

Sprinkle the cornflour and glutinous rice flour over the chicken and mix well.

Pour cooking oil into a 28cm (11¼in) frying pan (skillet), preferably cast iron, to fill it about halfway. Scrape off as much spice paste as possible from the chicken and set it aside. Fry the chicken in two batches at 150–160°C (300–320°F).

CONTINUED . . .

AYAM GORENG BEREMPAH CONTINUED . . .

Fry for 2 minutes, then turn the pieces over and fry for 1 minute. Cover the pan with the lid and reduce the heat. Cook, covered, for 4–7 minutes (depending on the size of the pieces). Remove the lid and invert it immediately, then use a dish towel to wipe the interior to remove the condensation. Turn the chicken over, replace the lid and cook for 3–6 minutes. Lift off the lid, increase the heat slightly and cook uncovered for 2 minutes. Turn the pieces over and cook for 2 minutes, then drain the chicken on a cooling rack placed over a tray.

After frying all the chicken, fry the reserved spice paste. Add the paste to the hot oil and cook at 160°C (320°F). It will sizzle a lot initially, then the sizzling will calm down. Stir often, so the paste browns evenly, and as it crisps up and starts to harden, break it into smaller pieces. Fry the paste until it's medium–dark brown, then scoop it out of the oil and drain on paper towels. Add the curry leaves to the hot oil and fry until crisp.

Place the chicken on a serving dish and add the curry leaves and half of the spice paste crumbs. Serve the remaining spice paste crumbs on the side.

JORDY NAVARRA'S FRIED CHICKEN

Serves: 4–6

4–6 fresh whole chicken legs, with the
    drumstick and thigh attached at the joint
about 90ml (6 tbsp) Filipino fish sauce
30g (1oz) cake or pastry flour
30g (1oz) cornflour (cornstarch)
about 750ml (3¼ cups) cooking oil
Maldon sea salt
banana ketchup, to serve

I'll admit to being sceptical about this recipe when chef Jordy Navarra sent it to me – it looked too easy. I should have had more faith in him, though. Jordy is the chef behind one of my favourite restaurants in Manila, Toyo Eatery, and, in 2018, won the Miele One to Watch award given to up-and-coming chefs by the Asia's 50 Best Restaurants Academy.

Jordy explained that this dish was inspired by two places in Manila that are famous for their fried chicken: Max's Restaurant and Classic Savory. Jordy made this dish when he was in Hong Kong for a guest chef promotion in 2019, and he sang the praises of local Hong Kong chickens, saying they have great flavour and are the perfect size – about 1.2kg (2lb 9oz). I agree – the first time I made this dish I used a whole Hong Kong chicken. But only the legs are used (the breast meat turns out too dry when cooked this way), so now I buy fresh whole chicken legs, which I debone myself. Deboned legs sold in supermarkets are sometimes misshapen and have all the leg's tendons still attached. If you do it yourself, you'll do a much tidier job. This chicken goes very well with the Tomato and Salted Egg Salad (page 171).

Jordy serves the chicken with his house-made banana ketchup, which is a long process because he even makes his own banana vinegar. I use commercial banana ketchup, which you can find in shops specializing in products from the Philippines. While you're there, buy Filipino fish sauce, which is essential to this dish. It's very different from Thai and Vietnamese fish sauce.

It's important to use non-stick pan coating (cooking spray) to spray the rack the chicken is cooled on – it works better than oil at preventing the meat from sticking.

Take the drumstick in one hand and the thigh in the other and bend the pieces backwards so the joint cracks. Put the chicken leg skin-side down on the cutting board. Starting at the thigh, use a paring knife to cut straight down to the bone. Run the knife down the entire length of the thigh bone, ending at where the thigh meets the drumstick. Use the tip of the knife to cut the meat away from the joint and bone without cutting the skin. Carefully cut the tendon at the joint between the drumstick and thigh, then take the now-clean thigh bone in your hand and twist it so it detaches from the rest of the leg.

CONTINUED . . .

BONE-IN THIGHS, DRUMSTICKS & WHOLE BIRDS

125

Run the paring knife down the entire length of the drumstick bone. Use the tip of the knife to cut the meat away from the top joint – where the thigh bone was. You'll see long white tendons – pull them out if you can. Scrape the meat away from the drumstick bone until you reach the tip. Use a cleaver to chop off the tip, then pull the drumstick bone away from the meat. You should have a fairly neat rectangle of meat and skin. Repeat with the remaining legs.

Use a pastry brush to brush fish sauce liberally over the legs – meat and skin – to cover them entirely.

Place the chicken pieces skin side-up in one layer on a tray that will fit into a steamer; you will probably need to do this in batches. Add enough water to the bottom of the steamer so that it comes to just under where the tray will sit. Bring the water to the boil, then carefully place the tray with the chicken pieces in it. Alternatively, if you do not have a steamer, place a low rack in a wok on which you can sit the tray of chicken. Cover with a lid and steam over a low heat for 20 minutes.

Spray a rack with non-stick pan coating (cooking spray). When all the chicken has been steamed, lay the pieces skin side-up on the rack set over a tray. Refrigerate, uncovered, for at least 4 hours.

Mix the cake (or pastry) flour with the cornflour. Dredge the chicken in the mixture to cover it entirely, then shake off the excess.

Pour cooking oil into a pan, preferably a medium wok, set over a medium heat, to fill it about halfway. Working in batches, place the chicken skin-side down in the hot oil. Fry at 160°C (320°F) for 2 minutes, then drain the chicken on a rack placed over a tray. Let the chicken rest for 5 minutes.

Heat the oil again, then fry the pieces at 170°C (340°F) for 1 minute to crisp up the skin.

Sprinkle Maldon salt over the chicken skin, then serve with banana ketchup.

KOREAN FRIED CHICKEN WITH YUJA TEA

Serves: 4–6

8–10 bone-in drumsticks and/or thighs, about 120–150g (4¼–5½oz) each
coarse salt flakes, as necessary
45g (1½oz) peeled garlic cloves
1 tsp finely ground white pepper
½ tsp granulated sugar
120g (4¼oz) coating mix (see page 162)
about 90ml (6 tbsp) iced water
about 150g (5½oz) potato, sweet potato or tapioca flour
about 750ml (3¼ cups) cooking oil

For the glaze
225g (8oz) Korean citron (yuja) tea (see intro)
50ml (generous 3 tbsp) rice vinegar
15ml (1 tbsp) soy sauce (all-purpose Kikkoman or your favourite brand)
10ml (2 tsp) sesame oil
toasted sesame seeds, as necessary

'Yuja' is the Korean word for yuzu, a fragrant, distinctive and delicious citrus fruit. In Korea, it's made into what's labelled as 'Citron Tea', although it doesn't contain tea leaves. Instead, Korean citron tea is like a thick, very sweet marmalade that's usually stirred into hot or cold water to make a refreshing drink. I use the citron tea to make a sweet-savoury glaze for chicken.

Double slash the chicken pieces on both sides, cutting all the way to the bone, and put in a bowl. Weigh the chicken, then multiply the amount by 0.005 – this is the amount of salt you need. Sprinkle the salt over the chicken and mix well. Mince the garlic, then mix it into the chicken along with the pepper and sugar. Marinate in the fridge for at least 4 hours.

Add the coating mix and the iced water to the bowl of chicken and mix well to create a batter that coats the pieces lightly and evenly. If necessary, adjust the consistency by mixing in more iced water. Dredge the battered chicken pieces in the potato, sweet potato or tapioca flour. Shake off the excess flour, then lay the chicken pieces on a cooling rack that's been placed over a tray. Leave the chicken to air-dry for at least 10 minutes.

Pour cooking oil into a 28cm (11¼in) frying pan (skillet), preferably cast iron, to fill it about halfway. Heat the oil, then fry the chicken in two batches at 150–160°C (300–320°F). Fry the chicken for 12–15 minutes, turning over the pieces as necessary. Take the chicken out of the pan and drain on the rack placed over the tray. Let the chicken rest for at least 10 minutes.

Heat the oil again, then fry the chicken at 170°C (340°F) for 2 minutes, turning over the pieces once. Drain the chicken on the rack.

While the chicken is frying the second time, make the glaze. Put the citron tea, vinegar, soy sauce, sesame oil and 30ml (2 tablespoons) warm water in a saucepan and place it over a medium heat. Stir well, then simmer until it reaches a light coating consistency.

Put half of the hot chicken in a bowl and pour over half the glaze. Toss the pieces in the bowl so they are very lightly coated with the glaze. Sprinkle with sesame seeds, then put the pieces on a serving plate. Repeat with the remaining chicken and glaze, sprinkle with sesame seeds and serve.

SOUTHERN THAI STREET-FOOD FRIED CHICKEN

8–10 bone-in drumsticks and/or thighs, about 120–150g (4¼–5½oz) each

30g (1oz) coriander (cilantro) roots with about 2.5cm (1in) of stem (see page 14)

30g (1oz) peeled garlic cloves

120ml (½ cup) fish sauce

20g (4 tsp) oyster sauce

30g (2 tbsp) granulated sugar

2 tsp finely ground white pepper

1½ tsp ground coriander

1½ tsp ground cumin

about 120g (4¼oz) coating mix (see page 162)

about 150g (5½oz) sweet potato flour

about 750ml (3¼ cups) cooking oil

When I made this chicken for a lunch party, a friend from Bangkok disputed my claim that this was really a Thai dish, because she hadn't ever tasted it before. Another Thai friend said that, actually, it does taste right, but pointed out that it was more of a southern Thai dish, with its use of cumin. Unfortunately, I haven't travelled enough outside of Bangkok to know the differences in Thai regional cuisines, but I do know this dish tastes good, especially with a simple, fresh Cucumber Salad (see page 168) on the side.

Double slash the chicken pieces on both sides, cutting all the way to the bone. Roughly chop the coriander roots and garlic, then put them in a mortar and pound to a paste with the pestle. Put the paste in a bowl and add the fish sauce, oyster sauce, sugar, and the ground white pepper, coriander and cumin. Spoon this mixture over the chicken and massage it into the meat, then marinate in the fridge for 8–24 hours, mixing occasionally.

Sprinkle the coating mix over the chicken and mix to create a batter that coats the pieces lightly and evenly. If necessary, mix in more coating mix or some iced water to adjust the consistency. Dredge the battered chicken in sweet potato flour, shake off the excess, then lay the pieces on a cooling rack placed over a tray. Leave to air-dry for at least 10 minutes.

Pour cooking oil into a 28cm (11¼in) frying pan (skillet), preferably cast iron, to fill it about halfway. Heat the oil, then fry the chicken in two batches at 150–160°C (300–320°F). Fry the chicken for 12–15 minutes, turning over the pieces as necessary. Take the chicken out of the pan and drain on the rack placed over the tray. Let the chicken rest for at least 10 minutes.

Heat the oil again, then fry the chicken at 170°C (340°F) for 2 minutes, turning over the pieces once. Drain the chicken on the rack, then pile the pieces on a plate and serve.

FRIED AFRICAN CHICKEN

~~~~~~

Serves: 4–6

8–10 bone-in drumsticks and/or thighs, about 120–150g (4¼–5½oz) each

coarse salt flakes, as necessary

about 120g (4¼oz) coating mix (see page 162)

about 150g (5½oz) tapioca flour

about 750ml (3¼ cups) cooking oil

For the spice paste

60g (2oz) peeled shallots

30g (1oz) peeled garlic cloves

15g (½oz) peeled ginger

50g (1¾oz) red banana chillies

15g (½oz) coriander (cilantro) root with about 2.5cm (1in) of the stem (see page 14)

12–20 red bird's-eye chillies

15g (1 tbsp) granulated sugar

10g (2 tsp) salt

1 tsp Tianjin chilli powder

½ tsp paprika

1 tsp medium-grind black pepper

30ml (2 tbsp) rice vinegar

15ml (1 tbsp) fish sauce

15ml (1 tbsp) fresh lime juice

60ml (¼ cup) canned coconut milk

African Chicken isn't actually from Africa. Rather, it's a dish that was created in Macau – a former Portuguese colony (now a Special Administrative Region of China) that's an hour away from Hong Kong by ferry. Over the centuries, cooks in Macau created some unique dishes, one of them being African Chicken (named so because of the spices), of which there are at least two popular versions. One is like a roast chicken with a spicy marinade, the other is chicken pieces in a rich, spicy sauce. As far as I know, there is no African Chicken that's fried. Until now. I took the flavours and used them to make a marinade that seasons the meat, and which is then used as the liquid in the batter that coats the chicken before it's fried. You won't find this dish on any restaurant menu in Macau, so you'll have to make it yourself.

Double slash the chicken pieces on both sides, cutting all the way to the bone, and put in a bowl. Weigh the chicken, then multiply the amount by 0.01 – this is the amount of salt you need. Sprinkle the salt over the chicken and mix well, then set aside while preparing the other ingredients.

For the spice paste, roughly chop the shallots, garlic, ginger, banana chillies and coriander root and put them in a blender (preferably a high-speed blender). Cut the bird's-eye chillies into thin rings, shaking out and discarding the seeds as you go. Put the chillies in the blender and add the sugar, salt, chilli powder, paprika, pepper, rice vinegar, fish sauce and lime juice. Purée the mixture until it's as smooth as possible, then mix in the coconut milk. Pour this mixture over the chicken, massage it into the meat and marinate in the fridge for 8–12 hours, mixing occasionally.

Add the coating mix to the bowl holding the marinated chicken and mix to make a batter that clings to the meat. If necessary, add more coating mix or some iced water, to adjust the consistency. Dredge the battered chicken in the tapioca flour and lay the pieces on a cooling rack placed over a tray. Leave them to air-dry for at least 10 minutes.

Pour cooking oil into a 28cm (11¼in) frying pan (skillet), preferably cast iron, to fill it about halfway. Heat the oil, then fry the chicken in two batches at 150–160°C (300–320°F). Fry the chicken for 12–15 minutes, turning over the pieces as necessary. Take the chicken out of the pan and drain on the rack placed over the tray. Let the chicken rest for at least 10 minutes.

Heat the oil again, then fry the chicken at 170°C (340°F) for 2 minutes, turning over the pieces once. Drain the chicken on a rack, then pile onto a plate and serve.

BONE-IN THIGHS, DRUMSTICKS & WHOLE BIRDS

AYAM GORENG MAMAK

~~~~~~ **Serves: 4–6**

8–10 bone-in drumsticks and/or thighs,
    about 120–150g (4¼–5½oz) each
coarse salt flakes, as necessary
40g (1½oz) rice flour
40g (1½oz) cornflour (cornstarch)
about 750ml (3¼ cups) cooking oil

For the spice paste
40g (1½oz) peeled garlic
20g (¾oz) peeled ginger
1½ tbsp Tianjin chilli powder
10g (⅓oz) curry powder
10g (⅓oz) ground turmeric
2 tsp ground coriander
2 tsp finely ground white pepper
10g (2 tsp) granulated sugar
60g (2oz) full-fat yogurt
40g (1½oz) egg white
6 x 10cm (4in) stalks of curry leaves

In Malaysia, 'mamak' indicates food made by Indian Muslims. At mamak stalls, the cooks lay out an array of prepared dishes for diners to pick and choose as they like. Except for the breads, much of the food is meant to be eaten at room temperature, including this fried chicken dish. Like some of the other highly spiced chicken dishes, including Ayam Goreng Berempah (see page 123), African Chicken (see page 133) and Fire Chicken (see page 76), this dish tastes better after it's been sitting out for at least a couple of hours because the flavours have time to develop.

Serve the chicken with steamed rice and sliced raw cucumber, which refreshes the palate.

Double slash the chicken pieces on both sides, cutting all the way to the bone, and put into a bowl. Weigh the chicken, then multiply the amount by 0.01 – this is the amount of salt you need. Sprinkle with the salt and mix well.

Roughly chop the garlic and ginger, then put them in a blender or food processor. Add the chilli powder, curry powder, ground turmeric and coriander, pepper, sugar, yogurt and egg white and blitz to a paste.

Remove the curry leaves from the stalk and mix them into the paste. Add the paste to the chicken and rub it into the meat. Marinate in the fridge for at least 4 hours.

Sprinkle the rice flour and cornflour over the chicken and mix well.

Pour cooking oil into a 28cm (11¼in) frying pan (skillet), preferably cast iron, to fill it about halfway. Fry the chicken in two batches at 150°C (300°F). Fry for 2 minutes, then turn the pieces over and fry for 1 minute. Cover the pan with the lid and reduce the heat. Cook, covered, for 4–7 minutes (depending on the size of the pieces). Remove the lid and invert it immediately, then use a dish towel to wipe the interior to remove the condensation. Turn the chicken over, replace the lid and cook for 3–6 minutes. Lift off the lid, increase the heat slightly and cook uncovered for 2 minutes. Turn the pieces over and cook for 2 minutes, then drain the chicken on a cooling rack placed over a tray.

Pile the pieces onto a plate and serve.

MARGARITA FORÉS' FRIED CHICKEN WITH GRAVY

For brining and frying the chicken
1.9 litres (8½ cups) water
100g (3½oz) coarse salt flakes
50g (generous 3 tbsp) brown sugar
2 tsp garlic powder
6–8 bone-in drumsticks and/or thighs,
 about 120–150g (4¼–5½oz) each
about 750ml (3¼ cups) cooking oil

For the seasoned coating mix
60g (2oz) plain (all-purpose) flour
65g (2oz) cornflour (cornstarch)
¾ tsp five-spice powder
1½ tsp garlic powder

For the gravy
15g (½oz) unsalted butter
15g (½oz) plain (all-purpose) flour
240ml (1 cup) chicken stock (see note)
60ml (¼ cup) full-fat milk
½ tsp soy sauce
 (all-purpose Kikkoman or your
 favourite brand)
¼ tsp medium-grind black pepper

Note
The gravy recipe calls for chicken stock. I use broth made from a bouillon cube, but if you have homemade stock, it will be even better. Bouillon cubes vary in saltiness, depending on the brand. If using, dilute the bouillon to half the strength, and, if necessary, adjust the saltiness of the gravy by adding more soy sauce (which also deepens the colour) or salt.

I was talking about my love for Jollibee's fried chicken with Margarita Forés, a chef in the Philippines who specializes in Italian cuisine with her restaurants Lusso, Grace Park and Alta. I commented that I wished I could have the Jollibee recipe for this cookbook, and she offered me this one, hastening to add that it's not an official recipe from Jollibee, but her version of their chicken. I'll admit, the flavours are not the same, but it's still very good fried chicken, and, like the Jollibee version, is served with a flavourful gravy.

The recipe uses a technique that is new to me: after the chicken is dredged in the coating mix, it's dipped quickly in water, then dredged again. I was sceptical – I thought the dip in the water would just wash off the coating, but it didn't. Instead of using plain water, I dip the chicken in the brine.

To make the brine, pour the water into a large bowl, then add the salt and sugar. Stir until completely dissolved, then mix in the garlic powder. Add the chicken pieces, then leave to brine in the fridge for 4–8 hours.

To make the gravy, melt the butter in a pan set over a low heat, then add the flour. Stir with a whisk for about 2 minutes over a low heat to create a pale brown roux. Add the chicken stock about 60ml (¼ cup) at a time, whisking well after each addition to make sure there are no lumps. When all the chicken stock has been added, whisk in the milk, then season with the soy sauce and black pepper. Bring to the boil, then simmer for a few minutes, or until it reaches the right consistency. Taste the gravy and adjust the seasonings if necessary. Turn off the heat.

Whisk the flour for the coating mix with the cornflour, five-spice powder and garlic powder. Take the chicken out of the brine and dredge each piece with the coating mix to coat it completely. Quickly dip the coated chicken in the brine, then dredge it again in the coating mix. Lay the pieces on a cooling rack placed over a tray and leave them to air-dry for at least 10 minutes.

Pour the cooking oil into a 28cm (11¼in) frying pan (skillet), preferably cast iron, to fill it about halfway. Heat the oil, then fry the chicken in two batches at 150–160°C (300–320°F). Fry the chicken for 12–15 minutes, turning over the pieces as necessary. Take the chicken out of the pan and drain on the rack placed over the tray. Let the chicken rest for at least 10 minutes.

Heat the oil again, then fry the chicken at 170°C (340°F) for 2 minutes, turning over the pieces once. Drain the chicken on the rack.

Reheat the gravy until hot. If necessary, thin it out by whisking in some water. Serve the gravy on the side with the chicken.

NOR MAI GAI

≈≈≈≈≈≈≈≈≈≈≈≈≈≈≈≈≈≈≈≈≈≈≈≈≈≈ **Serves: 4–6**

1 fresh chicken, without the head and feet,
  about 1.2kg (2lb 9oz)
coarse salt flakes, as necessary
cake or pastry flour, as necessary
light soy sauce, as necessary
cooking oil, for frying

For the rice
30g (1oz) dried Chinese mushrooms
  (see page 12)
30g (1oz) dried prawns (shrimp)
200g (7oz) glutinous rice
100g (3½oz) jasmine rice
½ tsp coarse salt flakes
120g (4¼oz) Chinese sausage (lap cheong,
  see page 11)
30g (1oz) spring onions (scallions)

This is by far the most difficult recipe in this book – it takes two days to prepare. It's not for the squeamish because it starts with tunnel-boning a chicken – removing all the bones (except from the wings) from a whole chicken, without cutting into the skin. The bird is then stuffed with glutinous rice, steamed to fully cook it, then air-dried before being double-fried. It's a dish for a very special occasion, to be served to friends who will notice and appreciate the hard work that went into it.

I first heard about this dish from my mother, who reminisced about eating it at a wedding banquet when she was a child – it made such an impression on her that she never forgot about it. She said that restaurants no longer make it because it is so involved. When I moved to Hong Kong, I went out for dim sum with some friends, and one of them ordered Nor Mai Gai (sticky rice chicken). I was thrilled that I would finally be tasting what my mother described. But it was nothing like it: technically it was Nor Mai Gai but it was far simpler: a small chunk of chicken with glutinous rice and Chinese mushrooms, wrapped in lotus leaf and then steamed.

So, I taught myself how to make it. The hardest part is tunnel-boning the chicken – it takes me at least 30 minutes (with practice). If you prefer, search out an old-fashioned butcher who is willing to do it for you, although they'll almost certainly charge a pretty penny for it. Or you can debone chicken wings (see page 61) and stuff them with the rice mixture. While good, the results are not nearly as impressive.

The rice is steamed then mixed with air-dried Chinese sausage (lap cheong), dried mushrooms and Chinese dried shrimp. The mushrooms take several hours to rehydrate – I soak them and the dried shrimp together. Be sure to save their soaking liquid to use as part of the liquid to cook the rice.

You need only about half the rice mixture for one bird. To heat the leftovers, you can either steam or microwave the rice or pan-fry in some oil (or lard, or rendered chicken fat), flattening it in the pan and cooking it until it's crusty.

It's important to use non-stick pan coating (cooking spray) to spray the metal skewers, the rack you put the bird on to steam and chill, and the other rack (if using another one) for frying the chicken. You want to make sure the chicken doesn't stick to anything, or the skin might tear.

CONTINUED . . .

The day before, briefly rinse the mushrooms and dried shrimp, then put them in a bowl, add 240ml (1 cup) cool water and soak until fully hydrated, at least 3 hours. Take the mushrooms and shrimp out of the water and squeeze them to extract as much liquid as possible and set aside. Strain the soaking liquid through a fine sieve placed over a bowl.

Put the glutinous rice and jasmine rice in the bowl of a rice cooker (or large bowl), place it on a scale and set the scale to zero (this is so you know how much water to add later). Rinse and drain the rice several times, or until the water is almost clear, then drain off most of the water. Put the bowl of rice back on the scale – it will be heavier because of the rinsing water. Pour in the mushroom/shrimp soaking liquid, then add fresh water so the total water weight (including the rinsing water) is 360ml (12½fl oz). Leave to soak while tunnel-boning the chicken.

Place a slightly damp dish towel on the work surface and a large cutting board on top (the towel will prevent the board from sliding around). Cut off the tip and middle joint of the wings, leaving the drumette attached to the bird. Put the chicken neck-side up on the board. With your fingertips, feel around in the cavity until you find the wishbone. Use your fingers to scrape away the flesh from the wishbone. Break the wishbone from where it is attached to the carcass at the base of the 'V', then pull it out of the cavity. Hold the drumette portion and wiggle it around to feel where it meets the shoulder, then use a paring knife to cut between the two joints within the cavity of the bird. Repeat with the other drumette. Take care not to pierce the skin.

Working within the cavity, scrape the flesh from the collarbones and shoulder bones. Snap the bones from the carcass, then pull them out of the cavity. Use your fingers to scrape away the flesh of the backbone, removing the meat and skin as close as possible to the carcass. The flesh along the back is very thin, so be careful that you do not damage the skin. When you get to the halfway point, snap off the top half of the back and pull it out. Turn the chicken over, so that the breast-side is up on the cutting board. Use your fingers to remove the breast meat as close as possible to the carcass, taking care not to damage the skin. When you get to the halfway point, snap off the top half of the breastbone and pull it out.

Continue to work on the breast side, scraping away the meat until the breastbone is bare and you're able to pull it out of the cavity. Turn the chicken over, and finish scraping the meat from the carcass on the lower half of the back. At the point where the back meets the thigh, use a paring knife to cut between the joint within the cavity. Again, working within the cavity, cut off the backbone from the tail and pull out. The chicken should be inside out.

CONTINUED . . .

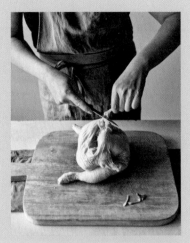

Scrape away the flesh from the thigh bone until you reach the drumstick. Cut the joint between the thigh and drumstick bones, then pull the thigh bone out of the carcass. Repeat on the other side.

Use a paring knife to cut the tendons around the circumference of the top of the drumstick. Scrape the flesh away from the drumstick bone until you reach the tip of the drumstick. The drumstick will be turned inside out – use a cleaver to chop off the bone from the inside, close to the tip. Repeat on the other side.

Weigh the now boneless chicken (except for the wing drumettes), then multiply the amount by 0.01 – this is the amount of salt you need. Sprinkle the salt over the inside of the bird, using more at the thick, fleshy parts, and less where the meat is thin. Turn the chicken so it is skin-side out, place it on a tray and refrigerate.

Mix ½ teaspoon of salt into the rice and water. Put the bowl holding the rice and water into the rice cooker, turn it on and cook until the rice is done. If you don't have a rice cooker, cook it on the stove top: put the rice and soaking liquid in a pan with a tight-fitting lid. Place over a high heat and bring to the boil. Reduce the heat to low, cover the pan, and cook until done. This method might need a little more water. Keep the rice hot.

Quarter the sausage lengthways, then dice it. Trim off and discard the stems from the Chinese mushrooms, then cut the caps into small dice. If the dried prawns are large, cut them into small pieces. Mince the spring onions. Set aside.

Put the sausage in a cold, unoiled frying pan (skillet) and place it over a medium heat. Cook until the fat starts to render out and the sausage starts to brown. Add the mushrooms and dried prawns and cook for about 3 minutes, stirring almost constantly. Mix in the spring onions. Add this to the cooked rice and mix well. Cool to room temperature.

Use non-stick pan coating (cooking spray) to spray four short, sharp metal skewers and a rack with feet that's large enough to place the chicken on, but will fit in your steamer.

Take 360g (12¾oz) of the rice mixture (refrigerate the remainder) and stuff it into the cavity of the bird, making sure there's some in the drumstick and thighs, and that it's in an even layer in the carcass. Use the skewers to secure the two openings in the bird, then place it breast-side up on the rack. Put the rack on a tray.

Put a small rack with feet in the bottom of a large wok and add enough hot water so the level is just under the rack. Bring to the boil over a high heat. Place the chicken – on the rack that's sitting on the tray – on the small rack in the wok. Drape a dry dish towel over the chicken (to catch the condensation), then put the lid on the wok. Steam over a high heat for 30 minutes. If necessary, pour more hot water into the wok so it doesn't dry out. Turn off the heat and leave covered for 25 minutes, then cool to room temperature.

Place an inverted plate over the chicken, then, holding the plate and rack together (with the chicken in between) quickly but carefully invert it all at once. Take care, because the chicken is very fragile at this point. Lift away the rack, then lightly and evenly dust the bottom of the chicken with cake or pastry flour. Brush with a thin layer of light soy sauce then replace the rack. Again, holding the plate and rack together, invert it so the chicken is once again breast side-up. Lift away the plate, then dust the bird with more cake flour and brush with more light soy sauce.

Clear a shelf in your fridge and cover it with paper towels. Put the chicken, still on the rack (but not on the tray), on the shelf – there needs to be air circulation around it and under it so the bird dries out. Refrigerate it uncovered for at least 8 hours, so it firms up and the skin is dry.

Before frying the chicken, carefully transfer it to a round rack or perforated pan (sprayed first with non-stick pan coating) that will fit in your pot. The pot should be straight sided, 24cm (9½in) or slightly larger in diameter, and at least 12cm (4½in) deep. Tie strings at three or four points around the round rack or pan, joined securely at the top, so you can lift the chicken in and out of the pot. Remove the skewers – twist them to loosen them, then pull them out.

Pour oil into the pot to fill it two-thirds of the way and place over a medium heat. Lower the chicken into the pot and fry it at 150–160°C (300–320°F) for about 8 minutes. If the bird is browning too fast, lift it out of the pot occasionally. If the top is not submerged in the oil, ladle the hot oil over it almost constantly.

After frying the chicken, let it rest at room temperature for 30 minutes. Reheat the oil, then lower the chicken into the pot and fry at 170°C (340°F) for 2 minutes, ladling oil over the top, if necessary. Cool for 10 minutes.

To carve the bird, use a very sharp, long knife to slice it in half from the top to the tail, then cut it into thick slices.

Variation

To serve as stuffed chicken wings, debone some wings as instructed on page 61. Stuff about 20g (¾oz) of filling into each wing, then secure the opening with a sturdy wooden toothpick that has been sprayed with non-stick pan coating (cooking spray). Dredge the wings with cake or pastry flour, then brush with light soy sauce. Place on a rack and air-dry in the fridge for at least 2 hours.

Fry the wings at 160°C (320°F) for 6 minutes. Rest at room temperature for 10 minutes, then fry again at 170°C (340°F) for 2 minutes. You will need about 18 wings for 360g (12¾oz) of the rice stuffing.

OIL-BLANCHED CHICKEN

~~~~~~~~~~~~~~~~~~~~~~~~~~~~~~~~~~

In the Chinese technique of oil-blanching, ingredients – usually meat, but it can be seafood – are marinated before being deep-fried briefly, sometimes for just 30 seconds or less. The marinade contains a starch – usually cornflour (cornstarch) – that lightly coats the ingredient and helps to protect it from the hot oil. The quick dip in the hot oil isn't enough to cook the ingredient; rather, it sets the exterior and gives it a lovely, smooth texture, which is why the technique is also known as 'velveting'. The ingredient is then cooked further, usually by stir-frying.

Oil-blanching is a popular technique in restaurants, but many home cooks are reluctant to do it, probably because it uses a fair amount of oil (although of course the oil can be reused, see page 22) and it can be messy. The amount of cornflour is quite small – certainly not enough to form a thick protective batter barrier. Instead, it just slightly thickens the marinade, but it remains pretty wet, and when the food hits the oil, it sizzles madly.

To help contain the splatters, I oil-blanch the ingredients in smaller amounts at a time and use less oil than called for in most of the other dishes in this book. I do this in a large wok, instead of the medium wok I use for most frying. This way, when the oil splatters, most of it will land within the wok.

For several of these dishes, I like to start with a whole, fresh chicken. The chicken is cut into smaller pieces for a stir-fry, so that when it's served, the diners can pick up the chunks of the bone-in meat with chopsticks. If you buy the chicken from a Chinese butcher, the shop will (or should) offer this service for free. Cutting it up like this at home is difficult unless you are skilled with a knife – or rather, a cleaver – because you need to chop up the bird through the bones into neat, evenly sized pieces, and the breastbone, especially, is very hard. If there's no Chinese butcher near you, or if the price of fresh chicken is exorbitant, it's better to use bone-in thighs that you cut through the bones into three pieces, or the mid-joint and drumette portions of chicken wings.

When stir-frying, certain fragile aromatics are cooked briefly to brighten up the colour, then removed from the wok and set aside while the chicken is cooked and the sauce is reduced. If the aromatics were to cook in the wok through the whole process, they would lose their texture and bright colour. Or, if they were simply added to the wok at the end, when the other ingredients are almost cooked, they would be just coated in the sauce, and wouldn't have the nice, glistening, vivid colour from being stir-fried with oil.

CHICKEN WITH BLACK BEAN SAUCE

Serves: 4–6

1kg (2lb 4oz) fresh chicken (without the head and feet), cut up for stir-frying, or chicken wings (separated at the joint), or bone-in thighs, each cut into 3 pieces through the bone

50ml (generous 3 tbsp) soy sauce (all-purpose Kikkoman or your favourite brand)

20ml (4 tsp) rice wine

5g (1 tsp) granulated sugar

5g (1 tsp) coarse salt flakes

1 tsp finely ground white pepper

20g (¾oz) cornflour (cornstarch)

10ml (2 tsp) sesame oil

50g (1¾oz) fermented black beans (see page 12)

1 red (bell) pepper, about 250g (9oz)

1 yellow (bell) pepper, about 250g (9oz)

125g (4½oz) peeled onion

8–10 spring onions (scallions)

3–5 peeled garlic cloves

2–4 thin slices of peeled ginger

2–4 red bird's-eye chillies

500ml (2 cups) cooking oil

Chinese fermented black beans have a very intense umami flavour that somehow complements all types of ingredients. Chicken with black bean sauce is a popular restaurant dish that's easy enough to make at home. Serve with steamed rice and stir-fried greens.

Put the chicken pieces in a bowl and add 30ml (2 tablespoons) of the soy sauce, the rice wine, sugar, salt and white pepper. Mix thoroughly, then stir in the cornflour and sesame oil. Leave to marinate for at least 30 minutes, stirring often.

Briefly rinse the fermented black beans, then put them in a small bowl and add 100ml (scant ½ cup) warm water. Leave to soak for at least 15 minutes.

Cut the red and yellow peppers into 1cm (½in) squares. Halve, then slice the onion. Cut the spring onions into 2.5cm (1in) lengths. Slice the garlic cloves and julienne the ginger. Cut the bird's-eye chillies into thin rings, shaking out and discarding the seeds as you go. Strain the black beans through a sieve (strainer) placed over a bowl; reserve the liquid. Stir the remaining 20ml (4 teaspoons) soy sauce into the soaking liquid. Roughly mash the black beans with the tines of a fork. Set aside.

Pour the cooking oil into a large wok set over a medium heat. Stir the chicken mixture to redistribute the cornflour (which sinks to the bottom) then fry at 160°C (320°F) in six or seven batches. As soon as you put the chicken in the oil, stir the pieces with chopsticks to separate them, and cook each batch for 1 minute. Use a slotted ladle to scoop the chicken out of the wok and drain on a cooling rack placed over a tray.

After frying all the chicken, pour off all but about 45ml (3 tablespoons) of oil from the wok. Place the wok over a high heat and, when it's hot, add the peppers and onion. Stir-fry until the peppers start to blister, then add the spring onions. Stir-fry until the spring onions brighten, then remove all the ingredients from the wok, leaving behind as much oil as possible.

Place the wok (no need to wash it) over a medium–low heat. Add the garlic and ginger and stir-fry for about 15 seconds, then add the bird's-eye chillies and crushed black beans and mix briefly. Increase the heat to high and stir in the chicken pieces, then pour in the black bean liquid/soy sauce. Stir well, bring to the boil, then reduce the heat to medium–low. Cover the wok with the lid and simmer for 5 minutes, stirring often.

Remove the lid and increase the heat to high. Simmer the ingredients for about 3 minutes, or until the sauce lightly coats the chicken, mixing often.

Season the sauce to taste. Add the peppers, onion and spring onions back into the wok, stir for about 30 seconds, then scoop the ingredients onto a plate and serve.

CASHEW CHICKEN

≈≈≈≈≈≈≈≈≈≈≈≈≈≈≈≈≈≈≈≈≈≈≈≈≈≈≈≈≈≈≈≈≈ **Serves: 4–6**

800g (1lb 12oz) boneless chicken breast

coarse salt flakes, as necessary

30ml (2 tbsp) soy sauce
  (all-purpose Kikkoman or your
  favourite brand)

20ml (4 tsp) rice wine

5g (1 tsp) granulated sugar

1 tsp finely ground white pepper

20g (¾oz) cornflour (cornstarch)

10ml (2 tsp) sesame oil

200g (7oz) peeled onion

2 red (bell) peppers, about 600g (1lb 5oz)
  in total

60g (2oz) spring onions (scallions)

2–4 peeled garlic cloves

2–4 slices of peeled ginger

60g (¼ cup) oyster sauce

20ml (4 tsp) rice vinegar

1 tsp medium-grind black pepper

500ml (2 cups) cooking oil

300g (10½oz) unsalted cashews

I think of this as a Chinese–American dish – something that you would order from places in shopping malls, where the signage is in faux Chinese font, and the paper chopstick covers have pictorial instructions on how to use them. At these restaurants, the best part of a dish of Cashew Chicken is the cashews – to the point where we used to clash chopsticks fighting to get them – but there were never enough. This version of the dish has plenty.

Butterfly the chicken breasts (see page 20), cut them into 1.25cm (½in) pieces and put them in a bowl. Weigh the chicken, then multiply the amount by 0.01 – this is the amount of salt you need. Sprinkle the salt over the chicken, then mix well. Set aside for at least 30 minutes.

Add the soy sauce, rice wine, sugar and white pepper to the chicken and mix. Stir in the cornflour and sesame oil, then leave to marinate for at least 30 minutes, mixing often.

Cut the onion and peppers into 1cm (½in) pieces. Cut the spring onions into 2.5cm (1in) lengths. Thinly slice the garlic cloves and julienne the ginger. Put the oyster sauce, vinegar and 100ml (scant ½ cup) water into a bowl and stir to combine. Put the black pepper and 5g (1 teaspoon) of salt into a small dish.

Pour the cooking oil into a large wok set over a medium heat. Add the cashews and fry at 150°C (300°F) for about 1 minute, or until toasted. Take them out of the oil, then drain on paper towels.

Heat the oil again. Stir the chicken mixture to redistribute the cornflour (which sinks to the bottom) then fry at 160°C (320°F) in six or seven batches. As soon as you put the chicken in the oil, stir the pieces with chopsticks to separate them, and cook each batch for 30 seconds. Use a slotted ladle to scoop the chicken out of the wok and drain on a rack placed over a tray.

After frying all the chicken, pour off all but about 45ml (3 tablespoons) of oil from the wok. Place the wok over a high heat and, when it's hot, add the onion and peppers. Stir-fry until the peppers start to blister, then add the spring onions. Stir-fry until the spring onions brighten, then remove all the ingredients from the wok.

Place the wok (no need to wash it) over a medium–low heat. Add the garlic and ginger and stir-fry for about 15 seconds. Increase the heat to high, then add the chicken and the oyster sauce mixture. Bring to the boil, then cook over a high heat for about a minute until the sauce lightly coats the chicken, stirring almost constantly. Add the bell peppers, onion and spring onions back to the wok and mix well. Sprinkle the black pepper and salt mix around the ingredients (not over them) and mix in. Taste the sauce and correct the seasonings, if necessary.

Stir in the cashews, then transfer the ingredients to a plate and serve with steamed rice and stir-fried vegetables..

SICHUAN CHICKEN POT

Serves: 4–6

8–12 dried Tianjin chillies
1–2 cinnamon sticks
1 whole nutmeg
3 star anise
4–6 red bird's-eye chillies
30g (1oz) chunk of peeled ginger
90g (3oz) Chinese celery (see page 14)
90g (3oz) spring onions (scallions)
20g (¾oz) fresh coriander (cilantro), with
   the stems and roots (see page 14)
15–20 peeled shallots
15–20 peeled garlic cloves
1 tbsp Sichuan peppercorns
4 green cardamom pods
1 tsp whole black peppercorns
1 tsp whole fennel seeds
1 tsp whole cumin seeds

For marinating and frying the chicken

30g (1oz) Chinese chilli sauce (see intro)
60g (2oz) doubanjiang (spicy fermented
   broad bean paste)
60g (¼ cup) oyster sauce
60g (2oz) chu hou paste (see intro)
30ml (2 tbsp) soy sauce
   (all-purpose Kikkoman or your
   favourite brand)
20ml (4 tsp) rice wine
15g (1 tbsp) granulated sugar
5g (1 tsp) coarse salt flakes
15ml (1 tbsp) sesame oil
1kg (2lb 4oz) fresh chicken (without the
   head and feet), cut up for stir-frying, or
   chicken wings (separated at the joint),
   or bone-in thighs, each cut into 3 pieces
   through the bone
20g (¾oz) cornflour (cornstarch)
530ml (2⅓ cups) cooking oil

Gai Bo (chicken pot) starts off life as one thing but ends up as something else. Bone-in chunks of chicken are mixed with a strong, spicy marinade, deep-fried, then cooked in a clay pot with a large array of whole aromatics that includes nutmeg, cinnamon stick, star anise, cardamom pods, garlic cloves and fennel seeds. After most of the ingredients are eaten, water or broth is stirred into what's left in the pot, and the flavourful liquid is used to poach ingredients for a hotpot.

This is a long list of ingredients, but cooking the dish is not difficult. Chinese chilli sauce comes in bottles; in Hong Kong, I am loyal to the sauce made by local producers, Yu Kwen Yick, but I've also made the chicken pot with ABC chilli sauce, which is made in Malaysia, or even Thai sriracha. Chu hou paste (also called chu hou sauce) is a condiment made from fermented soybeans. Doubanjiang is a salty, spicy and umami speciality of Sichuan province. If possible, buy Ceylon (Sri Lankan) cinnamon, also known as true cinnamon, which is far more delicate in taste and texture than the cassia bark often sold as cinnamon.

If you want a second 'course', add about 1.5 litres (6½ cups) of water or light broth to the pot after eating most of the ingredients. Bring to the boil on a portable tabletop burner and serve with raw ingredients such as thinly sliced beef, prawns, sliced fish, fresh mushrooms, lettuce and other leafy vegetables, and noodles.

To make the marinating/seasoning paste, mix the chilli sauce with the doubanjiang, oyster sauce, chu hou paste, soy sauce, rice wine, sugar, salt and sesame oil. Add 120g (4¼oz) of this paste to the chicken in a bowl, sprinkle in the cornflour and mix thoroughly. Marinate in the fridge for at least 4 hours, stirring often.

Pour 500ml (2 cups) of the cooking oil into a large wok set over a medium heat. Stir the chicken mixture, then fry it at 160°C (320°F) in six or seven batches. As soon as you put the chicken in the oil, stir with chopsticks to separate the pieces, and cook each batch for 1 minute. Use a slotted ladle to scoop the chicken out of the wok and drain on a cooling rack placed over a tray.

CONTINUED . . .

SICHUAN CHICKEN POT CONTINUED . . .

Briefly rinse the Tianjin chillies, then pat them dry. Tear them in half and shake out and discard the seeds. Break the cinnamon stick(s) in half. Wrap the nutmeg in a paper towel, then use the flat side of a metal meat mallet to crack it into several pieces. Wrap the star anise in a paper towel, then use the flat side of a metal meat mallet to break each one into several pieces. Bruise the whole bird's-eye chillies by hitting them with the side of a knife. Use the meat mallet to bash the ginger to break it lengthways into several pieces. Separate the leaves from the stalks of Chinese celery. Tear the stalks into 5cm (2in) lengths. Cut the spring onions into 2.5cm (1in) pieces. Separate the leaves from the stems and roots of the fresh coriander. Mince the stems and roots.

Pour the remaining 30ml (2 tablespoons) cooking oil into a clay pot or a saucepan that holds at least 2 litres (8¾ cups). Place the pot over a medium heat, add the whole shallots and garlic cloves and stir until lightly charred. Add the Tianjin chillies, cinnamon, nutmeg, star anise, bird's-eye chillies, ginger, Sichuan peppercorns, cardamom, black peppercorns, fennel and cumin seeds. Stir constantly for about 2 minutes to toast the spices. Add the remaining marinating/seasoning paste to the pot and stir constantly for 30 seconds – it will sizzle.

Add the chicken and 180ml (¾ cup) water. Bring to the boil, then cover the pot with the lid, reduce the heat and simmer for 20 minutes, stirring often. Remove the lid. The liquid should lightly coat the chicken pieces; if necessary, simmer over a high heat for a few minutes. Taste the sauce and correct the seasonings, if necessary. Mix in the celery stalks, spring onions, coriander roots and stems and simmer until wilted. Garnish with the celery and coriander leaves and serve immediately.

CHICKEN WITH DRIED MUSHROOMS & CHINESE SAUSAGE

Serves: 4–6

30g (1oz) dried Chinese mushrooms
  (see page 12)
1kg (2lb 4oz) fresh chicken (without the
  head and feet), cut up for stir-frying, or
  chicken wings (separated at the joint),
  or bone-in thighs, each cut into 3 pieces
  through the bone
30ml (2 tbsp) soy sauce
  (all-purpose Kikkoman or your
  favourite brand)
20ml (4 tsp) rice wine
5g (1 tsp) granulated sugar
5g (1 tsp) coarse salt flakes
1 tsp finely ground white pepper
20g (¾oz) cornflour (cornstarch)
10ml (2 tsp) sesame oil
180g (6¼oz) Chinese sausage (lap cheong,
  see page 11)
4–8 peeled garlic cloves
30g (1oz) peeled ginger
30g (1oz) spring onions (scallions)
500ml (2 cups) cooking oil

In a Cantonese household, this combination of ingredients is usually steamed, but I prefer to make it this way, because the chicken takes on an attractive golden hue from being fried, then braised.

Briefly rinse the dried mushrooms, then put them in a bowl and add 200ml (scant 1 cup) water. Leave to soak until fully hydrated, at least 3 hours.

Put the chicken pieces in a bowl and add the soy sauce, rice wine, sugar, salt and white pepper. Mix thoroughly, then stir in the cornstarch and sesame oil. Leave to marinate for at least 30 minutes, stirring often.

Slice the Chinese sausage on the diagonal. Halve the garlic cloves. Thinly slice the ginger and cut the spring onions into 2.5cm (1in) lengths. Take the mushrooms out of the soaking liquid and squeeze them to remove as much liquid as possible. Trim off and discard the mushroom stems, then thinly slice the caps. Strain the soaking liquid through a sieve (strainer), then measure out about 150ml (scant ⅔ cup). If there's not enough liquid, add some water.

Pour the cooking oil into a large wok set over a medium heat. Stir the chicken mixture to redistribute the cornflour (which sinks to the bottom), then fry at 160°C (320°F) in six or seven batches. As soon as you put the chicken in the oil, stir with chopsticks to separate the pieces, and cook each batch for 1 minute. Use a slotted ladle to scoop the chicken out of the wok and drain on a cooling rack placed over a tray.

Pour all but 20ml (4 teaspoons) of oil out of the wok and place it over a high heat. When the oil is hot, add the spring onions and stir-fry until they brighten. Take them out of the wok. Wipe the wok clean with paper towels.

Put the Chinese sausage in the wok and cook over a low–medium heat until some of the fat starts to render out. Increase the heat to medium–high and cook the sausage until it starts to char in spots. Mix in the ginger and garlic and cook for about 30 seconds. Stir in the chicken and mushrooms, then pour in the reserved 150ml (scant ⅔ cup) of the mushroom soaking liquid. Bring to the boil, then reduce the heat, cover the wok with the lid and simmer for about 15 minutes. Remove the lid, taste for seasonings and adjust, if necessary. Simmer the ingredients over a medium–high heat for about 3 minutes, or until the sauce lightly coats the chicken.

Add the spring onions back into the wok and stir well. Transfer the ingredients to a plate and serve immediately.

CHICKEN WITH SALTED CHILLIES, FERMENTED BLACK BEANS & CUCUMBER

Serves: 4–6

800g (1lb 12oz) boneless chicken breast

coarse salt flakes, as necessary

30ml (2 tbsp) soy sauce
(all-purpose Kikkoman or your
favourite brand)

20ml (4 tsp) rice wine

10g (2 tsp) granulated sugar

1 tsp finely ground white pepper

20g (¾oz) cornflour (cornstarch)

10ml (2 tsp) sesame oil

4 Asian cucumbers, about 120g
(4¼oz) each

30g (1oz) fermented black beans
(see page 12)

4–6 peeled garlic cloves

4–6 thin slices of peeled ginger

500ml (2 cups) cooking oil

20–30g (¾–1oz) salted chillies, homemade
or purchased (see below)

For the salted chillies

450g (1lb) red chillies – a mix of bird's-eye
and slender banana chillies (I use half and
half, but if you're a real chilli fiend, use a
proportion of 3:2)

45g (3 tbsp) coarse salt flakes

Note

*You can buy Chinese salted chillies in jars,
which might be labelled 'preserved chillies'
or 'pickled chillies'. The heat level varies from
brand to brand. I make them because it's easy
enough – although it takes about 2 weeks
before they're ready.*

**This dish was 'created' one day when I found a jar of salted chillies
(see note) that I had made, but forgotten about, so I decided to cook
them with chicken, and balanced their heat with chunks of cucumber.**

To make your own salted chillies, chop the chillies, discarding the stems and
most of the seeds. Mix the chillies with the salt, then put them into a sterilized jar
and cover tightly with the lid.

Leave at room temperature for 2 weeks, stirring occasionally with a sterilized spoon.
After 2 weeks, refrigerate the jar. This keeps for at least six months in the fridge.

Cut the chicken breasts into 1.25cm (½in) pieces and put them in a bowl. Weigh
the chicken, then multiply the amount by 0.01 – this is the amount of salt you need.
Sprinkle the salt over the chicken, then mix well. Set aside for at least 30 minutes.

Add the soy sauce, rice wine, 5g (1 teaspoon) of the sugar and the white pepper
to the chicken and mix. Stir in the cornflour and sesame oil, then leave to
marinate at room temperature for about 1 hour, mixing often.

Quarter the cucumbers lengthways and then cut into 1cm (½in) pieces. Weigh
them, then multiply the amount by 0.02 – this is the amount of salt you need.
Sprinkle the salt over them and mix well, then leave for at least 20 minutes.

Put the fermented black beans in a small bowl and add 60ml (¼ cup) water.
Leave to soak for at least 15 minutes.

Thinly slice the garlic cloves. Strain the black beans through a sieve (strainer)
placed over a bowl. Weigh the soaking liquid and add water to total 120ml
(½ cup). Add the remaining 5g (1 teaspoon) of sugar to the liquid and stir until
dissolved. Lightly crush the black beans with the tines of a fork. Drain the
cucumbers in a colander, then squeeze them with your hands to extract
as much liquid as possible. Set aside.

Pour the cooking oil into a large wok placed over a medium heat. Stir the chicken
mixture to redistribute the cornflour (which sinks to the bottom), then fry at
160°C (320°F) in six or seven batches. As soon as you put the chicken in the oil,
stir with chopsticks to separate the pieces, and cook each batch for 30 seconds.
Use a slotted ladle to scoop the chicken out of the wok and drain on a cooling
rack placed over a tray.

Pour off all but 20ml (4 teaspoons) of the oil, then place the wok (no need
to wash it) over a medium–low heat. Add the garlic and ginger and stir-fry for
about 15 seconds. Add 20g (¾oz) of salted chillies and the black beans and stir
for about 10 seconds.

Increase the heat to medium–high and add the chicken and the black bean soaking liquid and sugar mixture. Bring to the boil, then stir for 1 minute. Taste the sauce and correct the seasonings, if necessary. If it's too spicy, sprinkle in more sugar; if you want it spicier, mix in more salted chillies. Add the cucumbers and simmer for 1 minute. Scoop into a bowl and serve.

KUNG PAO CHICKEN

~~~~~~ **Serves: 4–6**

20g (¾oz) dried Tianjin chillies (use as
  necessary)
240g (8½oz) thin leeks or fat spring onions
  (scallions)
6–8 peeled garlic cloves
20ml (4 tsp) soy sauce
  (all-purpose Kikkoman or your
  favourite brand)
10g (2 tsp) granulated sugar
120ml (½ cup) Chinese brown rice vinegar
10ml (2 tsp) sesame oil
1 tsp cornflour (cornstarch)
4–6 thin slices of peeled ginger
4 tsp Sichuan peppercorns
180g (6¼oz) dry-roasted peanuts

For seasoning and frying the chicken
800g (1lb 12oz) boneless chicken breast
coarse salt flakes, as necessary
30ml (2 tbsp) soy sauce
  (all-purpose Kikkoman or your
  favourite brand)
20ml (4 tsp) rice wine
5g (1 tsp) granulated sugar
1 tsp finely ground white pepper
20g (¾oz) cornflour (cornstarch)
10ml (2 tsp) sesame oil
500ml (2 cups) cooking oil

Kung Pao Chicken is a dish you can find on the menus of Chinese restaurants everywhere (I think) in the world. But what you are served isn't necessarily the version you are familiar with. Some versions have a thick, gloopy sauce, others are very sweet, while some have lots of vegetables that don't belong in this dish. This version is somewhat austere compared to others, and I've been told that it tastes like the type you might be served in Beijing. Most recipes call for leeks, but they shouldn't be the very fat Welsh leeks. Buy leeks that are about 1.5cm (⅝in) in diameter – I like the ones from Japan. If you can't find those, buy the fattest spring onions (scallions) in the market.

Cut the chicken breasts into 1cm (½in) dice and put the pieces in a bowl. Weigh the chicken, then multiply the amount by 0.01 – this is the amount of salt you need. Sprinkle the salt over the chicken, then mix well. Set aside for at least 30 minutes.

Add the soy sauce, rice wine, sugar and white pepper to the chicken and mix. Stir in the cornflour and sesame oil, then leave to marinate at room temperature for about 1 hour, mixing often.

Briefly rinse the Tianjin chillies, then pat them dry. Tear each one into 2–3 pieces (depending on size), shaking out and discarding the seeds as you go. Weigh out 10g (⅓oz) of the chilli pieces. Slice the leeks (or spring onions) into 1cm (½in) pieces. Halve the garlic cloves. Mix the soy sauce with the sugar, rice vinegar, sesame oil and cornflour. Set aside.

Pour the cooking oil into a large wok set over a medium heat. Stir the chicken mixture to redistribute the cornflour (which sinks to the bottom), then fry it in six or seven batches at 160°C (320°F). As soon as you put the chicken in the oil, stir with chopsticks to separate the pieces, and cook each batch for 30 seconds. Use a slotted ladle to scoop the chicken out of the wok and drain on a cooling rack placed over a tray.

Pour off all but 20ml (4 teaspoons) of the oil, then place the wok over a low heat. Add the Tianjin chilli pieces and stir constantly, gently heating them until the colour brightens. Do not let the colour get too dark or they will taste acrid. Remove the chillies from the wok and set aside.

Place the wok over a medium–low heat and add the garlic, ginger and Sichuan peppercorns. Stir constantly until the peppercorns are toasted. Add the chillies, leeks (or spring onions) and chicken to the wok. Quickly stir the soy sauce/vinegar mixture to redistribute the cornflour and pour it over the ingredients. Increase the heat to medium–high and stir almost constantly for about 1 minute until the chicken is lightly coated with the sauce. Stir in the peanuts, then transfer to a plate and serve immediately.

OIL-BLANCHED CHICKEN

BASIC RECIPES

The coating you choose for fried chicken is what determines the texture of the crust. I never use wheat flour on its own, although plain (all-purpose) tends to be the preferred flour for fried chicken outside of Asia. For this book, I explored the wealth of flours on the supermarket shelves: tapioca, potato, sweet potato, rice, glutinous rice, corn and water chestnut. I didn't try using nut flours, or any grain flour that was too strongly flavoured, such as rye, because the coating should complement the chicken, not overwhelm it.

The flours I like most for fried chicken are potato, sweet potato and tapioca, which give a gentle crunch, medium crunch and hard crunch, respectively. These flours are sometimes labelled 'starch', and, if you try to research the differences between the two, most online posts will say that they are not the same and cannot be used interchangeably. I tested recipes with whatever I could get – potato flour and potato starch, sweet potato flour and sweet potato starch, and tapioca flour and tapioca starch – and couldn't discern any difference in taste or texture.

BASIC COATING MIX

It took much experimentation to figure out the correct proportions for this basic coating mix. My original recipe started off with more than 90% cake/pastry flour and just a little of any other type of flour. Now, it's only 40% cake flour, with the majority of the mix being potato, sweet potato or tapioca flour, depending on the type of crust I want – tapioca flour gives the hardest crunch while potato and sweet potato are softer. I make the coating mix in fairly small quantities, then store it in an airtight container. It will keep for at least three weeks but be sure to shake the container before using the mix, to redistribute the ingredients. If you're avoiding gluten, use gluten-free flour in place of the cake or pastry flour.

Whisk together both flours, then add the salt. Use a small sieve to sift the baking powder directly into the mixing bowl, then whisk again.

120g (4¼oz) potato, sweet potato or tapioca flour
80g (2¾oz) cake or pastry flour (or gluten-free flour)
5g (1 tsp) coarse salt flakes
1 tsp baking powder

BASIC COATING BATTER

A light, coatable batter uses approximately equal amounts of Basic Coating Mix (see above) and liquid (usually iced water). But you have to remember to take into consideration the liquid in the marinade, and even the liquid that comes out of the chicken when you salt it. When I mix the batter, I often add just a scant amount of iced water. The batter will be very thick initially, but it loosens up when it is mixed with the chicken. If necessary, I adjust the consistency by adding more iced water.

Add the iced water to the coating mix and whisk to combine. Pour over the chicken, then adjust the consistency, as necessary.

100g (3½oz) basic coating mix (see above), using your flour of choice
about 60ml (¼ cup) iced water

SUPER CRUNCHY BATTER

For the crunchiest coating of all – one that maintains its crunch (for a time) even when sauced (as in Strawberry Sweet and Sour Chicken on page 70 and Yangnyeom on page 35), I use even less water in the batter, and instead, I add oil and vinegar. Adding oil to batters is common in Chinese cuisine. I got the idea of adding vinegar when I made a fried version of Margarita Forés' chicken Inasal (see page 80) and noticed how hard and crunchy the batter was. You can adapt most of the recipes to have a harder crunch, by using this super-crunchy batter in place of the Basic Coating Batter (see above), which doesn't contain oil and vinegar. For the hardest, crunchiest batter, make the coating mix with tapioca flour.

Whisk all the ingredients together before mixing in with the chicken. If the consistency is too thick, mix in more iced water.

100g (3½oz) basic coating mix (see above)
40ml (2 tbsp + 2 tsp) iced water (use less if the marinade has a lot of liquid)
20ml (4 tsp) cooking oil
20ml (4 tsp) coconut vinegar or distilled white vinegar

CHICKEN STOCK & RENDERED CHICKEN FAT

There are several advantages to working with fresh, whole, local chickens. First is the taste and texture, of course. But there are also the off-bits that you don't get when using chicken parts, namely the bones and the fat. I collect both, store them in separate containers in the freezer, and when I have enough, make Chicken Stock and Rendered Chicken Fat. These are just guidelines, depending on how much of each you have.

CHICKEN STOCK

I make this plain, without any vegetables or herbs, so it can be used in any type of dish. If you make one that's strong on the rosemary and thyme, it won't work well for East and Southeast Asian dishes.

A stove-top pressure cooker or electric multicooker (like an Instant Pot) are fantastic at making relatively clear broths in only about 30 minutes. If you don't have either type of pressure cooker, simmer the bones over a low heat for about 2 hours.

Rinse the bones under cold running water, then put them in the pot of a pressure cooker or multicooker. Add enough water to cover by about 1cm (½in), then put the lid on and seal it. For stove-top pressure cookers, bring to high pressure, then reduce the heat and cook on high pressure for 30 minutes. With a multipurpose cooker, just press the soup or broth button and set it for 30 minutes.

Allow the pressure to cool naturally, then remove the lid. Pour the stock through a colander placed over a bowl and discard the bones. Cool to room temperature, decant the stock into containers that are a useful size to your household, then freeze for up to three months.

at least 500g (1lb 2oz) chicken bones, with some chicken feet, if possible
water

RENDERED CHICKEN FAT

Cut the skin and fat into small pieces, put them in a pan and add about 15ml (1 tablespoon) of water. Place the pan over a medium heat and bring to a simmer. Reduce the heat and cook at a low simmer until all the fat has rendered out, stirring often. Pour the fat through a sieve (strainer) placed over a bowl and cool to room temperature. Store the fat in an airtight container in the fridge for up to three months.

The chicken cracklings – the solid bits left in the sieve – are delicious. Crisp them up by baking them at 180°C/160°C fan/350°F/gas mark 4 until brown, then sprinkle with salt and let them cool. If you don't eat all of them immediately, they can be stored at room temperature in an airtight container for several days.

at least 250g (9oz) chicken skin and fat

ACCOMPANIMENTS

A person cannot live on fried chicken alone – you need something to eat with it! Here are just a few of my favourite accompaniments. You'll notice that several of the vegetable side dishes use cucumber. I love them because they are so refreshing. Be sure to seek out Asian cucumbers, which are quite small (about 120g/4¼oz each) and have thin skin and small, tender seeds. If you use larger cucumbers, you'll need to skin them and remove the seeds.

KOREAN PICKLED WHITE RADISH

This isn't the traditional way of making pickled radish. I was given the recipe by a Korean cook but misunderstood her instructions: I was meant to simmer the salt and sugar with water to create a brine, mix in the vinegar and pour this over the cubed radish. Instead, I made it the way I usually make pickles: by salting the vegetables first, then mixing in the other ingredients, in this case, distilled white vinegar and sugar.

The radish used in this recipe is the large, white variety known as icicle radish, 'daikon' (in Japanese), 'lo bok' (in Cantonese) or 'mu' (in Korean). If possible, use Korean mu, which is short, fat and sweet.

This pickled radish (pictured on page 169, top) goes well with all types of Korean fried chicken (see pages 35, 76 and 128).

Peel the radish, then cut it into 2cm (¾in) chunks. Weigh the radish and multiply the amount by 0.02 – this is the amount of salt you need. In a bowl, sprinkle the salt over the radish and mix well. Leave for about 30 minutes, or until the radish is softened.

Drain off most of the liquid. Put the radish in a sterilized glass jar, preferably one that's tall and narrow, so there's less surface area.

Add the sugar to the vinegar and stir to dissolve, then pour this over the radish. Seal the jar and refrigerate for at least 6 hours. These taste best if eaten within a week.

Serves: 4–8
as a side dish

300g (10½oz) white radish
  (see intro)
coarse salt flakes, as necessary
80g (⅓ cup) granulated sugar
120ml (½ cup) distilled white
  vinegar

VIETNAMESE PICKLED VEGETABLES

At Vietnamese restaurants, these carrot and white radish pickles are served as a side dish or are layered with other ingredients in Bánh Mì Thịt (Vietnamese sandwiches).

Peel the carrot and white radish and cut them into thick batons.

Proceed with the recipe as instructed for Korean pickled radish above.

Serves: 4–8
as a side dish

150g (5½oz) carrot
150g (5½oz) white radish
coarse salt flakes, as necessary
80g (⅓ cup) granulated sugar
120ml (½ cup) distilled white
  vinegar

SESAME GARLIC CUCUMBERS

'Smashed cucumbers' are now a popular side dish, even at non-Chinese restaurants, but these cucumbers are not smashed – instead, they're cut into neat pieces. The flavour is the same, though.

Weigh the cucumbers and multiply the amount by 0.02 – this is the amount of salt you need. Halve the cucumbers lengthways, then slice them on the diagonal about 1.25cm (½in) thick. Place in a bowl and mix in the salt and leave for about 30 minutes, or until they soften.

Drain the cucumbers, then use your hands to squeeze out as much water as possible. Blot the cucumbers with paper towels.

Mince the garlic and scatter it over the cucumbers. Add the sesame oil and mix well, then refrigerate for a few hours before eating.

Serves: 4–8
as a side dish

4 Asian cucumbers, about 120g
 (4¼oz) each
coarse salt flakes, as necessary
2–3 peeled garlic cloves
20ml (4 tsp) sesame oil

KIMCHI BASE

I keep a jar of this in my fridge at all times and use it whenever I'm in need of a quick batch of cucumber or white radish kimchi (see page 168) – I just salt the vegetables and add some of this kimchi base. The kimchi base uses saeujeot – tiny, salted shrimp sold in their brine. If you can't find it, add more anchovy sauce. If you can't find Korean anchovy sauce, substitute with Thai or Vietnamese fish sauce, although the flavour won't be the same.

Put the rice flour in a small pot, add 125ml (½ cup) water and whisk until smooth. Place the pot over a low heat and heat until simmering, stirring constantly. As soon as it comes to a simmer, turn off the heat and whisk in the sugar. Cool to room temperature.

Finely chop the saeujeot, garlic and ginger, then put them in a bowl. Add the rice flour mixture, gochugaru and anchovy sauce and stir until combined. Scrape into a sterilized jar, then refrigerate, and use as necessary. It keeps for at least 2 months.

Makes about 300g (10½oz)

20g (¾oz) glutinous rice flour
25g (5 tsp) granulated sugar
50g (1¾oz) saeujeot (see intro)
20g (¾oz) peeled garlic cloves
10g (⅓oz) thinly sliced peeled
 ginger
50g (1¾oz) gochugaru (Korean
 chilli flakes)
50ml (generous 3 tbsp) anchovy
 sauce

ACCOMPANIMENTS

167

CUCUMBER OR RADISH KIMCHI

I make cucumber and radish kimchi in small batches, because I like them when they are still relatively fresh, and not too aged. Make enough to eat within a week – how much that is depends on your household. I would count on using three-quarters to one cucumber (or about 100g/3½oz of radish) per person. If you have leftovers, just store them in a container in the fridge. If you're making both kimchis at the same time, don't combine the vegetables: they should be kimchi'd separately. (Radish Kimchi pictured opposite).

Weigh the cucumbers or peeled radish and multiply the amount by 0.02 – this is the amount of salt you need.

For cucumber kimchi, halve the cucumbers lengthways, then slice on the diagonal about 1cm (½in) thick. For radish kimchi, cut the radish into 2cm (¾in) chunks. Place in a bowl, sprinkle the salt over the vegetables and leave for about 30 minutes, or until softened.

Drain the cucumbers or radish, then use your hands to squeeze out as much water as possible. Blot the vegetables with paper towels.

Add a dollop of the kimchi base to the vegetables and mix well – there should be enough to lightly coat the cucumber or radish; if necessary, add more. Refrigerate for several hours before eating.

Make it according to your family size

2 Asian cucumbers, about
  120g (4¼oz) each, as necessary
white icicle radish, as necessary
coarse salt flakes, as necessary
kimchi base (page 167),
  as necessary

THAI CUCUMBER SALAD

My friend Tass – the amazing Thai home cook – says Thai salads can be made out of almost anything. She once made a salad out of some underripe cherries that were so tart I was about to throw them away. She also makes this tongue-tingling, refreshing cucumber salad. But the way she slices the cucumber makes me cringe, because I am terrified that she's going to cut herself. She holds the cucumber in one hand, and with the knife, chops down towards her hand, scoring the cucumber unevenly. She then slices off the cucumber shreds into a bowl. The uneven shreds – some fat and crunchy, others thin and more delicate – are texturally more interesting than perfectly even shreds, but for safety's sake, I recommend you cut the cucumbers on a cutting board.

Tass uses a type of 'cooked' fish sauce that's made specifically for Thai salads, but regular fish sauce is fine, too. She makes palm sugar syrup by simmering about three parts of palm sugar with one part water – this keeps in the fridge for weeks.

Cut the cucumbers into rough, uneven shreds.

Pound the garlic and chillies in a mortar. Halve the tomatoes, add them to the mortar and pound lightly, just to bruise them.

Mix in the fish sauce, sugar syrup, lime juice and shrimp paste. Taste for seasonings and adjust, if necessary. Mix in the cucumbers and dried prawns, then pile onto a plate and serve.

Serves: 2–4
as a side dish

2 Asian cucumbers, about
  120g (4¼oz) each
2–3 peeled garlic cloves
2–3 red bird's-eye chillies
6 cherry tomatoes
45ml (3 tbsp) fish sauce
5–10ml (1–2 tsp) palm sugar
  syrup
10–15ml (2–3 tsp) fresh lime juice
½ tsp shrimp paste, see page 43
  (optional)
5g (1 tsp) very small dried prawns
  (shrimp)

JAPANESE POTATO SALAD

When I was deep in the process of recipe testing, I would make a half-batch of this at a time, to eat throughout the week with whatever fried chicken I was making. Japanese Potato Salad goes well with many types of fried chicken, not just Japanese ones. The full recipe makes a lot – enough to feed at least 10 people as a side dish, but if your friends are like mine, they'll be happy to take leftovers home. To give this its distinctive flavour, you must use Kewpie mayonnaise – a Japanese mayonnaise that comes in a squeezy bottle.

Peel the potatoes, then cut them into 1cm (½in) cubes. Put the potatoes in a pan and add enough water to cover them by about 2.5cm (1in). Stir in 10g (2 teaspoons) of salt, then place the pan over a medium–high heat and bring to the boil. Reduce the heat and simmer the potatoes until they are very tender – they should be slightly overcooked but not falling apart.

Drain the potatoes but do not rinse them. Put them back in the pan used to cook them. Drizzle the vinegar over the potatoes, sprinkle with ½ teaspoon of salt, then mix well. It's okay if the potatoes get slightly crushed as you mix them. Set aside to cool completely – if you mix in the mayonnaise while they are still warm, the potato salad will look curdled.

To make the hard-boiled eggs, put the eggs in a small pan and add water to cover by 1cm (½in). Place the pan over a medium heat and bring to the boil. As soon as the water boils, turn off the heat and cover the pan with the lid. Leave for 12 minutes. Drain off the water, then put the eggs in a bowl of iced water to cool completely.

Halve the cucumber lengthways, then slice it as thinly as possible. Weigh the cucumber and multiply the weight by 0.02 – this is the amount of salt you need. Sprinkle the salt over the cucumbers and mix well, then leave for about 5 minutes. Drain the sliced cucumbers, then squeeze them with your hands to extract as much water as possible. Blot them with paper towels.

Crack the eggs, then peel them. Cut them into small dice.

Add the mayonnaise, eggs, cucumber and lots of pepper to the potatoes. Taste the mixture and add more salt and/or vinegar, if necessary. If the salad is dry and not creamy enough, mix in more mayonnaise. Chill for a few hours before serving.

Serves: 10–15
as a side dish

1kg (2lb 4oz) all-purpose
   potatoes
coarse salt flakes, as necessary
30ml (2 tbsp) rice vinegar
2 eggs
1 Asian cucumber, about
   120g (4¼oz)
at least 200g (7oz) Kewpie
   mayonnaise
lots of freshly ground black
   pepper

MAC SALAD

In California, my family had many friends and relatives from Hawaii who taught us the joys of Shave Ice (not 'shaved ice'), Lomi Lomi Salmon, Poke, Spam Musubi and Poi (fermented taro paste). My Japanese–Hawaiian aunt invariably brought Mac Salad whenever we went on a picnic or to the beach. It's important to slightly overcook the macaroni. If it's al dente, the mayonnaise won't absorb as well.

Bring a large pan of salted water to the boil, add the macaroni and cook until tender. Drain, rinse with cold water, then drain again.

Put the macaroni in a bowl and mix in the mayonnaise, vinegar, salt and pepper.

Use the large holes of a rasp-type grater to grate the carrot and onion. Mix them into the mac salad. Taste for seasonings and correct, if necessary. If it seems dry, mix in more mayonnaise.

Serves: 4–6
as a side dish

250g (9oz) elbow macaroni
at least 180g (6¼oz) Hellman's or
  Best Foods mayonnaise
15ml (1 tbsp) rice vinegar
¾ tsp coarse salt flakes
½ tsp medium-grind black
  pepper
30g (1oz) carrot
30g (1oz) onion

TOMATO & SALTED EGG SALAD

I first tasted this delicious salad about 10 years ago, at a dinner party in Manila, and have been making it ever since. I love it because it refreshes the palate between bites of meaty dishes. It goes well with Margarita Forés' chicken Inasal (page 80), Jordy Navarra's Fried Chicken (page 125), the Chicken Wings Relleno (page 65) and any of the 'dry' (without sauce) chicken recipes such as Ayam Goreng Berempah (page 123) and Lemongrass and Makrut Lime Leaf Chicken (page 87).

Be sure to use ripe, sweet cherry tomatoes for this dish. If the tomatoes are not sweet, mix in a small amount of granulated sugar, to balance the flavours.

In some countries, salted eggs are sold cooked, instead of raw. If you buy cooked salted eggs, skip the first paragraph.

Put the eggs in a small pan and add enough water to cover them by about 2.5cm (1 in). Place the pan over a medium heat and bring the water to the boil. As soon as the water boils, lower the heat, cover the pan with a lid and cook at a low simmer for 10–12 minutes, depending on the size of the egg. Drain off the water then rinse the eggs with cold water. When the eggs are cool, remove the shells.

Halve or quarter the cherry tomatoes, depending on size, and put them in a bowl. Add the salt and mix well. Halve the shallot and thinly slice it, then add the pieces to the bowl. Mix in the vinegar and, if necessary, add a little more salt and/or some sugar.

Use your fingers to break the eggs into small to medium roughly shaped pieces. Gently mix them with the tomatoes, then serve.

Serves: 4–6
as a side dish

2 salted duck eggs (see the note
  on page 50)
300g (10½oz) cherry tomatoes
½ tsp coarse salt flakes, or more
  if necessary
1 small peeled shallot
10ml (2 tsp) coconut or rice
  vinegar
granulated sugar, if necessary

ACCOMPANIMENTS

INDEX

INDEX

ACKNOWLEDGEMENTS

If eating well could be considered research, then I have been researching fried chicken – and all the subjects for my future cookbooks – for almost my entire life.

My parents, grandparents and various extended family members, especially my uncle Gene, started educating my palate when I was young, simply by cooking well, eating well, and generously sharing their food with others. A friend, listening to our family talk during a meal, said incredulously, 'You're still eating lunch and are already discussing what you will have for dinner!' There wasn't anything unusual about that because my family members – at least the ones I love best – had the philosophy that if you're going to eat, you should try to eat well. For that, and for their love and support, I give endless thanks.

I was food and wine editor at the *South China Morning Post* newspaper in Hong Kong for close to 25 years, and in that time, worked with a talented group of people that included editors, writers, photographers and food stylists. Thanks to Kevin Kwong, Winnie Chung, Meera Ganesan, Rachael Barker, Chris Wood, Mark Footer, Victoria Finlay, Enid Tsui, Vincenzo La Torre, Divia Harilela, Susan Sams, Jonathan Wong, Antony Dickson, May Tse, Nellie Ming Lee, Vhanya Mackechnie, and Joey Liu. Special thanks to Paul Buck, who noticed how well my fried chicken recipes did online and made the offhand remark, 'You should write a book about fried chicken.' I took the idea and ran with it.

I am lucky to have the most amazing network of supportive friends. In Hong Kong, I have to thank Desiree Au, Cathy Chon, Charmaine Chan, Lambda Li, Eileen Shen, Bettina Tan, Terri Ann Wong, Dorothy Chan, Fiona To, KC Fung, Enrica Tong, Peter Chang, Richard Feldman, Rose Leng, Dave Kunin, Deirdre Chan, Candice Suen Sieber, Yuda Chan, Jonathan Ah-weng, Keti Mazzi, Carol Joanna Lai, David Lai, the Diestel family, Margaret Lam, Danny Yip, Rose Leng, Yvonne Teh, Bessie Ng, Jeffrey Mui, Jefferson Liu, and my Hong Kong relatives, the Chu family.

Internationally, there's Anica Kim, Meei and François Gigandet, Jessie Ng, Annabel Betz, Evelyn Chen, Jung Yoon Choi, Rashmi Uday Singh, Amy Ma and Dominique Ansel, Daniel Calvert, Supapohn Kanwerayotin, Jan and Keith Oderberg, Daphne Romney KC, Jennifer Joan Lee, Hannah Raymond-Cox, Anna Katz, Tanya Yi, Jessica Chan, Grace Wong-Folliet,

Linda Wibowo, Thong Yoke-mei, Wai Yee Man, and my wonderful brother Greg Jung, equally-wonderful sisters-in-law, Hilary and Jill, and my nieces and nephews, Heather, Christopher, Nicholas, Lindsay and Matthew.

There are about a million chefs and restaurateurs I should thank publicly for feeding me so well and for inspiring my own cooking, but I know I will forget to mention someone and cause offence, so for now, I'll just call out the ones who helped me most with this book. The brilliant Elizabeth Chu of ZS Hospitality shared two excellent Vietnamese recipes. In Tokyo, there's Zaiyu Hasegawa, of Den, whose most famous creation, Dentucky Fried Chicken, opened my eyes to how creative one can be with the filling for stuffed chicken wings. In South Korea, Mingoo Kang, of Mingles, makes my favourite Korean Fried Chicken at his Hyodo Chicken shop in Seoul. I am thankful to two Manila-based chefs, Margarita Forés, whom I adore for several reasons, including her passion for food, for keeping me supplied with Taba ng Talangka (crab fat), and for the two recipes she contributed to this book; and Jordy Navarra, owner of Toyo Eatery in Manila, who also gave a recipe and answered my endless questions about it. Thanks also to Hong Kong-based chefs Anthony Ng (of Nikushou and Uza) and Steve Lee (of Hansik Goo) for our discussions about the serious subjects of coatings and frying temperatures for fried chicken. I am also extremely grateful to Tharinee 'Tass' Hosman, who taught me so much about Thai home cooking.

Thanks to Jill Dupleix, Clarissa Wei, Genevieve Yam, Ken Hom and Pat Nourse for reading *Kung Pao and Beyond*, and writing such nice comments about it.

A million thanks to Fuchsia Dunlop for her friendship, her advice on how to write a cookbook proposal, and for her introduction to the brilliant Quadrille team of Sarah Lavelle, Stacey Cleworth and Katy Everett. The photoshoots in London with Yuki Sugiura, Sam Dixon, Connie Simons, Kristine Jakobsson and Max Robinson were days of fun (and serious work) as they made my dishes look fantastic for the cookbook. Many thanks to Vicky Orchard and Sarah Epton for editing my words.

And, of course, loving thanks to my husband, Nigel Kat, who tasted various fried chicken recipes every day for about three months and didn't complain (too much) about it.

Susan Jung is the Food Columnist at *Vogue Hong Kong*. She was previously Food and Drinks Editor at the *South China Morning Post* for almost 25 years. Since 2014 she has been the Hong Kong, Taiwan and Macau Academy Chair for the World's 50 Best Restaurants and Asia's 50 Best Restaurants. She has travelled all over the world and has tried and tested every fried chicken recipe you could ever wish for.